Christianity Without Religion

"The Message That's Changing The World"

By Paul & Nuala O'Higgins

Paul and Nuala O'Higgins may be reached by writing to:
Reconciliation Outreach, Inc.
P.O. Box 2778
Stuart, Florida 33495

ISBN 1 (paperback) 978-0-578-06775-9

TABLE OF CONTENTS

FOREWORD

We have written this book for all who want to get to the real message of Christianity without dealing with the layers of cobwebs that often obscure it.

If religion is man's efforts to contact God through practices and rituals, then Christianity is not a religion at all. Religion is man's effort to reach God but Christianity is God's effort to reach us and reconcile us to Himself.

Many traditions have grown up around Christianity over the course of time. Christians have seldom lived up to the high standards of their calling. Throughout history they have fought with each other, competed with each other, insulted each other; and condemned and even killed the unbeliever.

Christianity has merged with the empires of history and the cultures into which it spread. Frequently, it has made business and even show business of its message. At times our motivation became so impure that the message was almost completely obscured. Politicians have manipulated it, businessmen have twisted it and entertainers have violated it. All of this has produced an ugly mixture, which is sometimes called "Christianity."

Real Christianity, however, is not this - it is the presence of God Himself moving among the peoples of this earth to communicate His love and life to them. It is God's love at work to reach the needy people in the world today. Above all it is His offer of a hope and a future for all. Christianity, therefore, is not a religion, nor just a message - it is a Person. Meet this Person and live. Meet the human systems built around this Person and if they do not bring you to Him, all you have met is mere religion.

When Jesus ascended to heaven He left His followers the benefit of His work, His word and His Spirit. His legacy is not a religion but HIS MESSAGE and HIS LIFE. The purpose of this book is to point to Him and His gift for you.

The title for this book is a paraphrase of the thought of Dietrich Bonhoffer, theologian and martyr who coined the phrase "religionless Christianity .

INTRODUCTION

"*These men are turning the world upside down.*" This was the report that was passed around concerning the first Christians. In fact, God *was* turning the world upside down through them. Today once again, and more than ever, God is using ordinary people to turn the world upside down.

For a brief moment the world saw the Glory of God in the person of Jesus. Now that Glory is becoming manifest in every corner of the earth as millions receive Him and yield themselves to Him to be His followers.

The call begins with an invitation to receive the mercy of God through the cross of Jesus. Our life with Him begins with a discovery of Jesus as the Door. It advances and grows with a life of obedience and union with Him as the Way. It will be perfected when His Glory swallows up all that is inglorious in us with His powerful presence at His return.

This process is taking place each day in the lives of individual believers, and also on a global scale throughout the earth as millions come to faith in The Messiah - Jesus.

The kingdom of God is here on the earth already. It is here now in a hidden way, like leaven in a batch of bread, or salt in the stew. The hour is coming soon when all that veils the Glory of God from being seen on the earth will fall asunder at Christ's return.

Jesus said *"The Glory which thou hast given me, I have given to them, that they may be one even as we are one, I in them and thou in me, that they may become perfectly one, so that the world may know that thou hast sent me and hast loved them even as thou hast loved me"* (John 17:22-23).

In these days this prayer is being answered. Millions of ordinary people today are presenting themselves to God that the life of Christ may come within them and that His Glory may be seen on the earth through them.

In this book, we seek to set forth some of the principles by which this great prayer of Jesus can be fulfilled in our lives. The days of mere church membership are over. The days when believers would come to Jesus for forgiveness and nothing more are over.

In these days tens of thousands are hearing the call to follow Him. The church is "rising" like Lazarus from the tomb and throwing off the binding grave cloths of tradition and fear to move into the earth showing forth the radiant love, compassion and character of Jesus. The Glory that the world saw through Him will be seen again when His face is seen in our lives.

As Jesus brought the power and presence and rule of heaven to bear into the darkness and suffering of earth, so today God's people are being mobilized by the Holy Spirit to make His Light shine, and His Glory seen in every part of the world.

Heaven is invading earth with its warmth and healing, first in Jesus, then through those that are born of Him and walk His way on earth. As those who have come to Him for forgiveness surrender further to bear His life and walk in His ways, then the His glory will be seen on the earth. The Glory that is already within believers is about to break forth in an unprecedented way on our earth. Heaven is coming to earth, first in Jesus, and now through Him in us and finally in full triumph on His return to Jerusalem in Glory.

CHAPTER 1

THE VERDICT - NOT GUILTY

W e are all aware that there is something wrong with us. Each day we are bombarded with information that reminds us of this fact. We are conscious of an uneasy guilty feeling within us. We think that perhaps this feeling would go away if we had a better job, a smarter home, a nicer car, or if we were not so fat, short, tall, skinny, underprivileged, over-privileged or anything else that we are not now.

Sometimes we think that this uneasy feeling would go away if we could kick over the traces of rigid convention or the ethical codes of our society, which we may regard as repressive. Others seek release from their internal disease by conforming themselves blandly to the culture they find themselves in. They try to find acceptance by doing all the "right" things, having all the "right" things and going all the "right" places.

None of these methods can erase that deep-seated feeling in all of us that something is the matter with us. This awareness just will not go away. All the money or success in the world, the entire social acceptance through conformity, fame or achievement, all the attempted escapes from conventional codes of morality and behavior cannot remove this sense that is deep-seated within everyone who comes into the world.

Preachers may tell us that what is wrong with us is that we are sinners. Usually that just makes us feel worse and even more hopeless and uneasy about our situation. We are not really interested in theological explanations. Oh yes, we do believe that God exists, but He is so impossible to please and so remote from our situation, we think it best to leave Him alone - if He will leave us alone.

> God has decided not to leave us alone. He loves us and wants to become involved in our lives.

However, God has decided *not* to leave us alone. He loves us and wants to become involved in our lives. Love would not be love if it did not reach out to help when it could. Love would not be love if it kept its distance when its closeness was needed. For this reason God has decided to involve Himself in our lives and in our history without violating the freedom He has given us to reject or to cooperate with Him and with His ways.

From the very beginning God has involved Himself in human history. At first He revealed Himself to Adam and to some of his descendants, then more fully to Abraham, his son, Isaac and Isaac's son, Jacob. Their descendants, the tribes of Israel, received a special call to be the receptors of the Word of God.

Through Moses God revealed His way more fully to His people. He showed them that the source of their problems was separation from Him and the consequence of this separation was death. He revealed to them a strict code of ethics and conduct that would be pleasing to Him, and keep them from harm. However, again and again, the people showed their inability to live by such high moral and spiritual standards.

God knew that it would not be enough for Him to reveal to us His high and holy standards. He would also have to make provision for us when we would fail to meet these standards. God knew He would have to give Himself fully in love without reservation to His creation, man, if He were to succeed in getting man to respond to Him in unreserved love. He would have to reveal something more than a moral standard. He would have to reveal His own Self.

"In many and various ways God spoke of old to our fathers by the prophets; but in these last days He has spoken to us by a Son, whom He appointed the heir of all things, through whom also He created the world. He reflects the glory of God and bears the very stamp of His nature, upholding the universe by His powerful word." (Hebrews 1:1-3). *"And the Word was made flesh, and dwelt among us, full of grace and truth; ... And from His fullness have we all received grace upon grace. For the law was given through Moses; grace and truth came through Jesus Christ. No one has ever seen God; the only Son, who is in the bosom of the Father, He has made Him known"* (John 1:14-16). *"For God so loved the world that He gave His only Son, that whoever believes in Him should not perish but have eternal life."* (John 3:16).

Two thousand years ago, God sent His only Son into the world. God became man as a Jewish carpenter in Nazareth called Jesus. This man, who was God as man, died at a place called Calvary on the Mount of Olives outside Jerusalem. He became our substitute, dying in our place and taking on Himself our sin and the consequences of all of our inadequacies.

Through Moses and the prophets, God had revealed that the consequence of sin - spiritual and moral unwholeness - is death. The Law and the prophets diagnosed our problem. However, it

was through Jesus that God provided the ⌐
prescription. God was sending Jesus into ⌐
world to take upon Himself the consequences of
our sin so that we could be acquitted.

*"The wages of sin is death - but the free gift of
God is eternal life in Christ Jesus."* (Romans
6:23)

- Through ourselves we earned death.
- Through Jesus we are offered forgiveness and
  life.

Isaiah had prophesied this great event over
seven hundred years earlier. *"All we like sheep
have gone astray, we have turned everyone to his
own way; and the Lord has laid on Him the
iniquity of us all. .... Yet it was the will of the
Lord to bruise him; He has put him to grief,
when He makes himself an offering for sin ...by
His knowledge shall the righteous one my
servant, make many to be accounted righteous;
and He shall bear their iniquities."* (Isaiah
53:6,10,11).

This amazing acquittal of the human race
by the sacrifice, which God Himself made
through Jesus, was accomplished for all of us
two thousand years ago. All that is required of us
now is that we

- recognize our need of it
- accept it
- and renounce everything that made us need
  forgiveness in the first place.

The Scales Of Justice

Imagine a great balance scale? On the one side are all of our sins, inadequacies and shortcomings that have us weighed down with a sense of guilt, frustration and unworthiness before God. Even the most upright among us are imperfect and fallen short of the standards of God. The best of us, no less than the worst of us, have enough on the debit side of the scale to tip it unfavorably against us.

As Paul puts it: *"All have sinned and all fall short of the glory of God."* (Romans 3:23). However, now we place the blood of Jesus on the other pan of the weighing scales. This perfect offering more than outweighs all the inadequacies and sins of both the worst of us and the best of us.

Spiritually, all our debts are paid in full by His great sacrifice for us. We are justified (acquitted*) "by His grace as a gift, through the redemption which is in Christ Jesus, whom God put forward as an expiation by His blood to be received by faith."* (Romans 3:24). The scales of justice have been eternally tipped in our favor by the work of Jesus on the cross!

Let us imagine a bottle of black ink spilt carelessly on a white table. The white table becomes black and stained. Now we take a sheet of pure white blotting paper and place it on the inky table. What happens? The table becomes white again and the blotting paper becomes black. The blotting paper has become black so that the table could become white again. The paper forfeits its own whiteness so that the table can regain its whiteness.

This is an exact parallel of what happens in the spiritual order when Jesus takes our sins upon Himself. He did this two thousand years ago, but it only becomes effective towards us when we apply its benefits to our lives through faith.

Paul puts it this way: *"For our sake He made him to be sin who knew no sin so that in Him we might become the righteousness of God."* (2 Cor. 5:21). God loves us so much that He sent Jesus to take our appointment with judgment so that anyone who accepts the provisions of Jesus' death does not come into condemnation. We lived, on death row, spiritually. Jesus came and took the execution for us so that we could go free without a record.

> *There are only two sorts of people on the earth: those whom God loves and those who know it!*

God accepts us into the realm of His love and grace not on the shaky ground of our goodness, but on the solid ground of the work of Jesus on the cross. Right standing with God is not a position one arrives at after years of religious activity, holy living, special meditation procedures or any such thing It is a gift already paid for that is freely available to every man, woman or child who will simply receive. Our relationship with God is not based on how good we are but on how forgiven we are!

There are only two sorts of people on the earth: those whom God loves and those who know it! There is no one that He does not love to the supreme extent that made Him willing to give His Son as a ransom for everyone and has done so.

Though the sacrifice of Jesus was offered once and for all for all of us, it does not benefit any of us until we put our faith in it. Just as a check is useless unless we cash it, or a tap cannot fill a cup unless the cup is turned upward to be filled, God's pardon is of no use to unless we receive it.

We Must Hear To Believe

We cannot put our faith in the sacrifice of Jesus unless we are told about it. The realm of God's love is like a great banquet that has been freely opened up to all of us through the work of Jesus on the cross, but not everyone knows that they can freely enter and eat.

Once there was a very wealthy man who decided to use his money to help the hungry people in a part of Africa that had been devastated with severe famine. He set up a large soup kitchen in one of the villages and spread the word around the region that whoever needed food could come and eat. Within a few weeks the hunger problem of the immediate area had virtually ceased. Only a few people in the area remained hungry. Most of these were people who, because of isolation, had not been told about the soup kitchen. There were also a few, who, though knowing that the food was freely available, were too proud to eat the food which the rich man had provided. These people were too proud to accept anything for which they could not pay.

The tragedy today is that while God's love has been made freely available to all, not everybody knows about it. There are some who

> *The tragedy today is that while God's love has been made freely available to all, not everybody knows about it.*

do know about it but refuse it preferring to attempt to make their way without God's assistance. There are some who do not know about the grace of God because they have never been told about it. Others hide from God, acting as if He did not exist or was not interested in them. Still others refuse to be in debt to God and believe that they can please Him and get near to Him on the grounds of their good morality and conduct. These people are like starving people

19

waiting to make themselves strong before they will approach the table for food.

This truth is also illustrated in the story of two young ladies who flew from a cold northern climate to the Caribbean for a winter vacation. They moved into their hotel room on the beach and their hearts rejoiced. They were going to spend the whole week on the beach soaking up the warm, friendly tanning rays of the sun and return to their northern city with a beautiful healthy-looking tan.

However, when they looked out their window at the tanned bodies of the other sunbathers, they were too ashamed to go on the beach in their bathing suits thinking they were too pale. As long as they remained in this fearful attitude, of course, they could never get a tan. Soon their desire to enjoy the sun overcame their shame of coming boldly into the sunlight. When they first came out onto the beach, indeed, they were the palest ones there. However, within a few days they were as tanned as anyone else there.

Many are afraid to come boldly into the light of God's wonderful love and grace because of a painful awareness of their inadequacy and unworthiness. If we wait until we are adequate or good enough, we will wait forever. If we do that, we would be like the pale sunbathers waiting until they are tanned before they appear in the sunlight.

Jesus has taken our sins and inadequacies on Himself so that we can come boldly into the realm of God's love and grace. *"Therefore, brethren, since we have confidence to enter the sanctuary by the blood of Jesus, by the new and living way which He opened for us through the curtain, that is through His flesh, and since we have a great priest over the house of God, let us draw near with a true heart in full assurance of faith..."* (Hebrews 10:19-21).

Jesus told a wonderful story about a young man who left home and spent all his money and energies on dissolute living. When he finally came to the pitiful end of his resources, he longed to return home but was quite fearful of doing so because of the disgraceful way that he had wasted his inheritance. When he finally did return home, his loving father treated him as if he had never done anything wrong and as if he had lived his whole life in complete perfection. (Luke 15)

This is how God receives all who return to Him through the provision of Jesus. No matter how dissolute our past life has been, He chooses not to remember our sins and to accept us as if we had lived our whole lives in complete perfection. God promises, *"I will remember their sins no more."* (Jer 31:34) How amazing is and grace! He is not holding our sins As we come to Him, He will cleanse ~~ all our mistakes and never remember them again. God has no second-class members in His family. We can all draw very close to Him. When and if we sin, we should not run FROM Him but TO Him allowing Him to love us, forgive us and change us.

"Justified by faith we have peace with God through our Lord Jesus Christ.... God's love has been poured into our hearts through the Holy Spirit, which has been given us." (Romans 5:1,6). How wonderful when we let God forgive us and allow Him to flood our hearts with His love through the Holy Spirit. God is not waiting for us to be good before He accepts us into His family and gives us the gift of right standing with Him. He offers us the gift of His love and forgiveness and perfect standing with Him no matter what state of life we may be in. Whether company president or skid row dropout, He makes the same offer freely to us all.

"While we were still weak, at the right time Christ died for the ungodly. Why, one will hardly die for a righteous man - though perhaps for a good man one will dare even to die. But God shows His love for us in that while we were yet sinners Christ died for us." (Romans 5:6-8)

There is no one on the face of the earth today, nor has there ever been, nor will there ever be, more loved by God than you are at this moment! Our only responsibility is to "soak it up" and respond to it.

> *There is no one on the face of the earth today more loved by God than you!*

Jesus has removed all barriers between this amazing love and us on the cross. Those who come to God can come through Jesus into glorious realms of grace.

Any attempt to approach the love of God apart from the work of Jesus will fail. The veil of our sinfulness makes it impossible for us to stand in the pure light of God's love apart from the covering that God Himself provided for us when He appointed Jesus to bear our sins.

When a criminal escapes from the law and evades justice, deep inside himself he never feels free before the world and, in particular, before the representatives of the law, no matter how benign or loving they may be. Inside, his heart condemns him. However, if he goes to court and confesses his crime and is subsequently acquitted through mercy or serves his sentence, he no longer has that sense of guilt and fear upon his release.

Those who attempt to approach God's grace apart from the work of Jesus can never know the deep peace and cleansing of those of us who have confessed our sins and accepted the fact that Jesus has taken our sentence so that justice is satisfied. The sacrifice of Jesus and the shedding of His blood satisfy the holy standards of a righteous God. Eternal cosmic justice is satisfied perfectly by the sentence that Jesus bore.

It is important to make note at this point that God did not demand the death of Christ for us as if He were some vengeful executioner. To the contrary, He Himself was humbling Himself for us in Jesus, bearing on Himself the consequences of our self-destructive behavior so that we could be acquitted.

"God was in Christ reconciling the world to Himself, not counting their trespasses against them" (2 Corinthians 5:19). Like a courageous mother who steps in to protect her child from the bullets of an insane gunman, so God interposed Himself in Jesus between our sins and us. By and large the full meaning of this amazing acquittal, which gives us justification or right standing with God, has not been fully appreciated and apprehended by most believers.

Righteousness Is Positive

Righteousness means much more than the forgiveness of our sins. It is not just something that takes care of the negatives of our lives, but it is a positive new position before God. Not only does God acquit us of our sins, He also lifts us up to share Jesus' very own relationship with Him. He adopts us into the royal family of heaven and puts the Spirit of Jesus into us. Not only does this King pardon His wrongdoer, He also makes him a part of His own royal family.

> *Not only does this King pardon His wrongdoer, but He makes him a part of His own royal family.*

We are not just "sinners saved by grace". We once were sinners, but now, through grace, we have been given a new nature, and the gift of right standing with God on the basis of Jesus' work. Jesus took all our unrighteousness and shame upon Himself on the cross and now offers us His righteousness - right standing with God - as a gift. Our task is to believe it, receive it and walk in it.

"He destined us in love to be His sons through Jesus Christ, according to the purpose of His will, to the praise of His glorious grace, which He freely bestowed on us in the Beloved. In Him we have redemption through His blood, the forgiveness of our trespasses, according to the riches of His grace which He lavished upon us" (Ephesians 1:5-8).

When God gives us the gift of righteousness, He takes our unrighteousness and places it on the Cross of Jesus, and He takes the righteousness of Jesus and places it on us! With this righteousness we can approach God and live in His presence with confidence! It is a totally undeserved gift. Most believers have failed to lay hold the awesomeness of this gift.

Jesus shares His Father with us making Him our Father, too. This puts us in a position of intimacy with God so that we too can call Him "Father!" *"And because you are sons, God has sent the Spirit of His son into our hearts, crying "Abba! Father! So through God you are no longer a slave but a son, and if a son, then an heir."* (Gal. 4:6-7)

This confidence that becomes ours in our relationship with God enables us to go through the rest of our lives with the happy awareness that we are continually surrounded by His love, care and benign activity. To be righteous, then, means much more than acquittal and forgiveness of our sins - it is the ability to stand in God's presence without any sense of inferiority, guilt or condemnation.

> *We can go through life with the happy awareness that we are continually surrounded by God's love, care and benign activity.*

"There is no fear in love, but perfect love casts out fear. For fear has to do with punishment, and he who fears is not perfected in

love." (I John 4:18). Believers in Jesus can confidently pray "in the Name of Jesus" because He has lifted us up to share in His own Sonship.

"His divine power has granted to us all things pertaining to life and godliness, through the knowledge of, Him who has called to His own glory and excellence, by which He has granted to us His precious and very great promises, that through these you may escape from the corruption that is in the world because of passion and become partakers of the divine nature." (2 Peter 1:3-4).

Each of us has the responsibility to personally appropriate this righteousness, which has been made available to all. To do this we must put our faith in God's plan through Jesus and come close to Him through Jesus' atoning work. Just as an entrance ticket to the theatre is worthless if the bearer does not use it to enter the theatre and attend the concert, so too the work of Jesus on the cross is of no avail to us unless we boldly put our faith in it and enter into a life of fellowship and closeness to God our Father.

Faith, then, is more than the intellectual belief in Jesus' work. It is the act of "using" what Jesus accomplished on the cross as the gateway to a life of undeserved blessings from God and allowing Him to love us as we respond to His love. The ticket holder puts his faith in the ticket, not when he accepts the ticket but when he uses it to enter the theatre.

Many people have a mere intellectual faith in the work of Jesus but are not really using it to enter into a life of fellowship with God. They are like ticket holders who have never entered the theatre. Let us be sure to enter the kingdom of God through the work of Jesus. This is our highest destiny and is the greatest thing that can happen to anyone. The experience of it is better than the reports of it!

A Prayer

Heavenly Father, thank you for sending Jesus to bear my sin and guilt on the Cross. I acknowledge my need of His great work and I put my faith in the fact that He has paid for my sins. Thank You that through Him I can come home to You, and to Your love and grace

I thank You, Jesus, for being my Savior. Through You I now approach Your Father as my Father. I ask You, Father, to let me experience Your love and Your grace at work in my life every day. I lay down the sinful side of my nature at the Cross of Jesus and I invite the Spirit of Jesus to come within me to empower me to walk in Your love and ways each day. Amen.

CHAPTER 2

TURN AROUND

W hen we hear the word "repent" most of us have an immediate tendency to hide or run away. We hope against hope that the challenge is not being directed to us. We associate the word with condemnation. Like naughty schoolboys seeking to hide from the accusing finger of the all-seeing schoolteacher, we fear the call to repentance. Jesus sounds the clearest call to repentance that the world has ever heard. Yet, He did not come to condemn the world, but to save the world, not to condemn sinners but to befriend and heal them.

The Good News begins with a call to repentance: *"Repent, and believe the good news. The time is fulfilled and the kingdom of God is at hand."* (Mark 1:15). These are the first words of Jesus that are recorded in Mark's gospel. *This* call to repentance is not the cry of the "finger pointer" but the cry of one who offers a great new beginning to mankind in general and every individual in particular. The call to repentance is a simple, direct call to change - to drop the old in favor of a far more wonderful way of living.

When salesmen advertise a new product that makes similar products obsolete, they are in fact calling us to repent from our old product, our old way of cleaning, or dressing, or eating, or whatever they are advertising, to a new and better way of doing that activity.

Similarly, the call to repentance is not just a negative call that criticizes and condemns our old way of living, but a call to accept a wonderful alternative to our old ineffective, self-destructive, self-orientated, self-dependent way of living. In fact, it is only when something better is presented to us that we can change from the old to the new. It is only when we actually see that the new is better that we can be willing to make the switch. To repent is to switch from an old way of living to a new way of living after the new way is discovered to be more desirable and better than the old way.

Once there was a young man who was the proud owner of a dilapidated old car. He was very attached to this car even though it was far

> *The call to repent is c call to accept a wonderful alternative to our old ineffective, self-destructive, self-orientated, self-dependent way of living.*

from being roadworthy. Indeed, his brothers referred to it as "an accident looking for a place to happen."

His friends constantly urged him to get rid of the disgraceful wreck, and his parents had become quite concerned that the car could bring about his death some day. Time went by and still the young man refused to heed his friends' and parents' warnings.

One day the young man's parents came up with a wonderful solution, though a costly one. They decided to buy him a brand new car and to give it to him as a gift. As soon as he saw the new car and was told that it was a gift from his loving parents, he was elated. "This is wonderful!" he exclaimed as he jumped in behind the wheel. From then on, he never drove or even thought about his old car again.

"The kingdom of heaven is like treasure hidden in a field", said Jesus, "which a man found and covered up; then in his joy he goes and sells all that he has and buys that field." "Again", He said, "the kingdom of heaven is like a merchant in search of fine pearls, who, in finding one pearl of great value, went and sold all that he had and bought it." (Matt. 13:44-45).

When we really see what the kingdom of God is really like we, too, will want to sell out. This is real repentance. We see repentance so much in negative terms that we miss the fact that it is essentially a call to accept something that is far more valuable and worthwhile than anything we may have to give up.

To repent means to change one's mind and heart. Our minds and wills can only be changed when they are presented with something that they perceive to be better than what they already have. Psychology has confirmed what was always suspected, that when there is a clash between our wills and our desires, our desires always "win." It is only when the desires are shown something more desirable that the will can choose to change.

The offer of the kingdom of God is the highest and most desirable offer we could receive. When faced with its claims, it is easy for us to leave our lower way of living as separated independent beings and change to a life of trust and friendship with God under His benign protection and provision.

Jesus preached this kind of repentance. He is not a nagging complainer but the joyful herald of good news. His voice calls us to come away from the insufficiencies of our separated lives into the all sufficiency of the love and care of God.

As we come to Him we must, of course, acknowledge the insufficiency of the old life, its inadequacy and its failure to deeply satisfy. But this is not hard to do when we are accepting something far better to replace it. The returning prodigal, who represents all of us who have gone our own way, is more conscious of returning to the shelter and love of his father than he is of leaving his old frustrating way of living.

> *Those who live 'good' lives and are respectable law-abiding citizens are in just as great a need of repentance as more obvious sinners.*

We often think of repentance as something that "bad" people need to do. We think of it as something that happens when "bad" people finally decide to straighten up, or when one of us decides to give up some bad habit. The repentance that Jesus calls us to, however, goes far deeper than turning from bad habits and ways.

He constantly pointed out that those who live "good" lives and are respectable law-abiding citizens are in just as great a need of repentance as more obvious sinners. He said: *"Truly, I say to you, the tax collectors and the harlots go into the kingdom of God before you. For John came to you in the way of righteousness, and you did not believe him, but the tax collectors and the harlots believed him."* (Matt. 21:31-32).

Jesus showed how difficult it is for people who are living "good" lives to recognize that they are in need of repentance. They find it hard to recognize their need of repentance because they are (they believe) doing all right and making a success of their lives apart from God's direct help.

"Bad" people, on the other hand, keep getting themselves into trouble and so are often quicker to recognize their need of God's mercy and help. They have discovered by experience that the life built on "self" is unsatisfying and unsatisfactory. And so they find it easier to abandon their independent self-propelled way of living, thrust themselves on the mercy and care of God and receive from Him the ability to live in a new way.

"Those who are well have no need of a physician, but those who are sick." (Mark 2:17). Those who do not realize that they are sick will never make themselves available to the healing work of the physician.

Repentance, then, is not merely changing from "bad" behavior to "good" behavior, but changing from a life that is lived by the power of SELF to a life that is lived in complete and total dependence on God. It is the change from a "self" life (whether that self is "good" or "bad") to a "Christ" life.

Real repentance goes beyond being aware that there is something wrong with our behavior and that we need God's forgiveness, to an admission that we need His Presence and life to uphold us in every area of our lives.

Jesus describes those who receive the kingdom of God as the "poor in spirit." The "poor in spirit" are those who know they cannot live without God and do not want to live without Him. Those who are deeply aware of their need of God are the kind of people who are ready for the kingdom of God.

Real repentance is totally different from any self-righteous resolve to do better or to pull ourselves up by our bootstraps. Only the Holy Spirit can bring it about. It only comes when we realize our total inability to meet God's standards for us apart from His mercy and continuous direct enablement.

We repent when we realize that our problem is deeper than our behavior and admit that we ourselves are the problem and not just our conduct. We can only repent in this way when we realize we fall short apart from God's direct presence and help in our lives. This is the switch of real repentance - not just changing from bad behavior to good behavior, but changing

- from lives empowered by self
- to lives empowered by God.

"Good" people need this kind of repentance as much as "bad" people.

Jesus promised to send the Holy Spirit to convict the world of sin. We are often too blind, complacent or self-sufficient even to realize that we ourselves stand in need of

- the mercy of God to forgive us,
- the grace of God to change us and
- the continuous presence of God to keep us.

In real repentance, we go far beyond the act of making good resolutions. When we acknowledge the inadequacy of our natural, self-powered lives, we can accept God's forgiveness and receive Jesus' life to come into us to empower us. We can then begin to live from the power of His presence with us and in us, rather than by the power of "self."

"Have mercy on me, O God, according to thy steadfast love; according to thy abundant mercy, blot out my transgressions. Wash me thoroughly from my iniquity, and cleanse me from my sin!"

> In God's kingdom there are no self-righteous people, but only those who realize that they cannot make it apart from the continuous gift of His mercy and the new life He gives.

"Create in me a clean heart, O God, and put a new and right spirit within me. Cast me not away from thy presence, and take not thy Holy Spirit from me." (Psalm 51:1-2,10-11)

In God's kingdom there are no self-righteous people, but only those who realize that they cannot make it apart from the continuous gift of His mercy and the new life He gives. Jesus said that apart from His continuous presence with us, we could do nothing (John 15:5). This means, He does not expect us to do anything or to be able to do anything apart from Him. When we discover that our lives have no lasting value apart from Him, we are ready to be joined to Him. As the finger cannot function apart from the hand, but becomes weak and lifeless, so we cannot function as our Creator intends us, as long as we remain separated from Him.

Repentance goes beyond simply changing our behavior. It consists in coming away from our separation from God. *"I am the true vine, "* Jesus says, *"and my Father is the vinedresser.... As the branch cannot bear fruit by itself unless it abides in the vine, neither can you unless you abide in me. I am the vine, you are the branches. He who abides in me, and I in him, he it is that bears much fruit, for apart from me you can do nothing. If a man does not abide in me, he is cast forth as a branch and withers; and the branches are gathered, thrown into the fire and burned."* (John 15:1,4-6)

When God asks us to repent, He is not scolding us, but calling us away from lives that are fruitless and spiritually withered. He is leading us from the loneliness of pride and self-sufficiency to receive the free forgiveness of sins. He is offering His love and His Spirit to equip us for a wonderful new life under the leadership of Jesus and in union with Himself.

A Prayer

Father forgive me for trying to make it on my own. I need You. I need Your forgiveness. I need Your presence and power to sustain me every moment of the day. I ask You to give me the new life of the Holy Spirit that I may no longer live from the "engine" of my own self, but from the "engine" of Your Spirit.

I ask you, Jesus, to take the "steering wheel" of my life that my life can be lived under Your control. I choose to no longer live for my own goals and ends but for You, and Your purposes. I renounce living by the power of my independent self and I come home to You, Father, to live the rest of my life under the shelter of Your care, provision and grace.

CHAPTER 3

REST FROM THE QUEST

German theologian, Dietrich Bonhoffer coined the phrase "religionless Christianity". There is much truth in the phrase. Although sociologists and others regard Christianity as a great religion, in fact, it is not a religion at all.

Religion is man's effort to bind himself back to God and to try to please God by improving himself through will power and other techniques. It is man's effort to reach up to God to find favor with Him. This can get us into bizarre activities and even lead to religious fanaticism. It leads ultimately to confusion and futility.

The Bible records the story of a group of zealous people who tried to reach God through their own efforts and energies. They set out to build a tower that reached to Heaven. Their project was built on their own zeal and ingenuity and was to be a monument to their own greatness and skill.

Then they said, *"Come let us build ourselves a city and a tower with its top in the heavens, and let us make a name for ourselves, lest we be scattered abroad upon the face of the whole earth". ... "And the Lord came down to see the city and the tower, which the sons of men had built. And the Lord said, "Behold, they are one people, and they have all one language; and this is only the beginning of what they will do, and nothing that they propose to do will now be impossible for them. Come let us go down, and there confuse their language, that they may not understand one another's speech." So the Lord scattered them abroad from there over the face of all the earth"* (Genesis 11:4-8).

The Babylonians are a symbol of all "self-made" men. They are examples of people who build their lives on their own strength and resources. God's kingdom is almost completely opposite to this. In His kingdom there are no "self-made" men, only those who have allowed God to make something out of their lives. The lives we try to make *for* ourselves *by* ourselves, and the life, which God makes for us in His grace and provision, are quite different.

> *Abraham is a symbol and model of all men of faith, whose life is a product of God's blessing rather than their own prowess.*

The book of Genesis also tells the story of Abraham. His life is in complete contrast to the Babylonian way. He is a symbol and model of all men of faith, whose life is a product of God's blessing rather than their own prowess. Abraham, in contrast to the men of Babylon, set out to follow God's plan. *"He looked for a "city which has foundations whose builder and maker is God."* (Hebrews 11:10). When God called him, He said to him: *"I will make you a great nation, and I will bless you, and make your name great, so that you will be a blessing"* (Genesis 12:2).

The "self-made man" is found pre-eminently in the business world but also in the world of religious pursuit. The Babylonians were, after all, trying to build a tower to reach to heaven. Much of what goes by the name of piety and religion today is simply the tower of Babel all over again ... that is, man by his own efforts and through his own skill and intelligence trying to measure up to God's heights.

The kingdom of God is such a contrast to all of this that, to many, it is a scandal and an affront. Jesus' kingdom is for the "poor in spirit", the meek and those hungering after righteousness. Those who receive His kingdom are people who are painfully aware of their need of God's mercy and grace. They are deeply conscious of their own inability to please God apart from the direct intervention of God Himself.

God's kingdom is not a plateau to which we can climb, but is something we receive from Him as a gift. It is God's radical is breakthrough into our lives to share His love and resources with us and to transform us into His likeness. It is for those who, like Abraham, are aware of the inadequacy of anything that is built simply on mere human effort. They have discovered that all our endeavors will come to confusion and frustration unless they have God at its foundation and builder, They know that we cannot please God unless God Himself stoops down to help us.

Today we live in an age of unprecedented confidence in our own systems and cleverness. There are signs, however, that this self-confidence is beginning to falter.

> *As the world is confronted anew with its limitations, God Himself can become more active in our world.*

Science, technology and social engineering have failed to bring Utopia. There is increasing uneasiness throughout the world as nations are faced with social and moral problems equal to those of any previous generation. The way of self-reliance - of thinking we can build our own paradise - is coming to a new point of confusion.

Politics, commerce, the social sciences, and religion are all limited in their ability to solve our problems. God, seeing the futility of Babylon, allows our prideful self-confidence reach its limitations. As the world is confronted anew with its limitations, God Himself can become more active in our world. He is most able to act as the Shaper of our destiny when we are most aware of our need of Him. When we turn away from self-dependence, we can receive from Him a blueprint of the new plan He has for our lives.

What has He in mind for our lives? We have tried (like the Babylonians) to make a name for ourselves, but what is the name He could make for us? What are the plans and projects and destinies into which He could cause us to come? God's says *"I know the plans I have for you, plans for welfare and not for evil, to give you a future and a hope.* (Jeremiah 29:11) His plans for us are far more wonderful than any plans we could make for ourselves. *" As it is written, what no eye has seen, nor **ear heard**, nor the heart of man conceived, what God has prepared for those who love him."* (1 Cor. 2:9)

When we discover what God wants us to be, we realize that by following Jesus we can become more than mere products of our culture and heredity. We can become products of His refashioning. Those who do not follow Him miss not only the kingdom of God but also the greatest adventure and romance on earth. Abraham discovered this when he left his Babylonian culture behind. The disciples discovered this on that great day in their lives when they came face to face with Jesus, who called them to

- follow
- forsake, and
- become.

Leaving Babylon

To the person who tries to build his life by his own power, repentance means to try harder and harder. It is no wonder that when we hear such calls to repentance, we almost instinctively recoil from them. Many "good" people who go to a church or synagogue, work hard every day, do not rob or commit adultery, pay their taxes and give some charitable donations, are so good that they do not see that they are in need of God's help. They don't realize that they need God's presence, life and power. As good as these people's lives are, they are not yet what God wants them to be. God has so much more for them.

Jesus told a story about two men who went to pray. *"He also told this story to some who trusted in themselves that they were righteous and despised others: "Two men went up into the temple to pray, one a Pharisee and the other a tax collector. The Pharisee stood and prayed thus with himself, "God, I thank thee that I am not like other men, extortioners, unjust, adulterers, or even like this tax-collector. I fast twice a week, I give tithes of all that I get."*

"But the tax-collector, standing far off would not even lift up his eyes to heaven, but beat his breast saying, "God be merciful to me a sinner!" "I tell you", said Jesus, "this man went down to his house justified rather than the other." (Lk. 18:9-14).

Many people have the idea that repentance is simply a matter of stopping "bad" activity and trying to do "good" things instead. This idea has done tremendous damage. Millions have been assured that they had repented when they had, in fact, simply become self-righteous.

There are millions who believe they are fully pleasing to God because they don't do obviously bad things. They are convinced that they have repented when in fact they have never really done so. They believe they are working FOR God and that they are doing their part for God and performing their duties as good citizens and good Christians.

They are like the builders of the tower of Babel. Their efforts are no more valuable to God than the efforts of the builders of that tower of confusion. They have never really repented, perhaps through no fault of their own, except that they trusted too much on themselves just like the Pharisee in Jesus' story.

As long as we are building on self, we have not repented. To repent is to look to the power, person and presence of God to act for us, with us, and through us, and to put no confidence in anything which has not had its origin in Him. Jesus said that everyone who heard and acted on His instructions would be like *"a wise man who built his house upon the rock; and the rain fell, and the floods came, and the winds blew and beat upon that house, but it did not fall, because it had been founded on the rock. And everyone who hears these words of mine and does not do them will be like a foolish man who built his house upon the sand; and the rain fell and the floods came, and the winds blew and beat against that house, and it fell; and great was the fall of it. "* (Matt 7: 24-27).

In his vision John saw Babylon had fallen (Rev. 18.2) and Paul warns believers to come out of Babylon and have no part in it. (2 Corinthians 6:17) Babylon here is not the literal city of Babylon because at the time of Paul and John, that city was already in ruins and nobody was living in it.

In the context in which John and Paul speak Babylon is not a place but a symbol for all the work and lives that are not built on the power of God and the rock of Christ. What is built on self is destined for destruction and confusion, like the tower of Babel, but what is built on God's Word and His promises (as Abraham's life was) will endure forever. The winds of time and the rains of adversity will not destroy what is built on God, His promises and the work of Jesus. God is still drawing to Himself people who, like Abraham, will build their lives on God's promises and not on themselves.

Today more than ever when technology has placed at our disposal such amazing resources, we should be unusually discerning in our assessment of religious movements. Size of crowds, financial success, and widespread reputation are no criteria for discerning whether any particular project has its origin in God or in man. The people at Babel were highly successful in what they were doing, but their project had its origin in man's pride, man's power and man's ingenuity.

> *God can use, the ingenuity of men; but when we act apart from Him, He considers our work to be nothing.*

God can use our skills and ingenuity, but when we act apart from Him, He considers our work to be nothing "*Apart from me you can do nothing,*" says Jesus (John 15:5). He considers anything done apart from Him and His help to be nothing, no matter how religious that project is.

Even the use of the name of God and Bible terminology is no guarantee that the project has God as its source. To add God's name to our projects will not make them His projects. To do this is to take His name in vain.

"Not everyone who says to me "Lord, Lord", shall enter the kingdom of heaven, but he who does the will of my Father who is in heaven. On that day many will say to me, "Lord, Lord, did we not prophesy in Your name and cast out demons in your name, and do many mighty works in your name?" And then will I declare to them, "I never knew you; depart from me, you evildoers" (Matthew 7:21-23).

These works and projects, even when they are religious have been done from the ambition and pride of man, are what the scriptures call "dead works". In these last days when we are warned that lawlessness would abound, the earth is filled with the clamor of these dead works. Such works bring with them a noisy and frantic activity - the same kind of noisy excitement and bustle that filled the city when the builders of Babel were at work.

Let us be careful that the feverish activity, which goes on in the Lord's name, does not seduce us, and let us not confuse it with the real work of the Lord. Two men can be involved in the same church or in the same Christian program, one of whom is there by the leading of the Spirit, and the other by the leading of his carnal ambition. One is involved in a 'dead work' and the other in a living ministry.

Let us leave Babylon. Leave activity that has its origin in our natural selves and be alive and attentive to do those things that proceed from God, building our lives on the foundation of His care and His promises.

"Follow Me and I Will Make You..."

When Jesus called His first disciples, He said to them what He says to you: *"Follow me and I will make you..."* (Mark 1:17). He was calling them to leave what they were in the world for the sake of what He could make of them. He was calling them away from the life they could make for themselves to the life He was choosing for them.

Those men, like you and us, were the product of their culture and their education, of their family life styles and their religious backgrounds. A sociologist could have made many projections about the way their lives would turn out. When these men encountered Jesus, the living Word of God, they were challenged to leave what they could make of themselves and what others expected them to make of themselves and follow Him and allow Him to make something altogether different of their lives.

The adventure of discipleship is that we learn to surrender our lives to the One who loves us most - God Himself. By following and forsaking we are refashioned and remolded by Him to be the kinds of people that He wants us to become. This life calls us to forsake all our "Babylons", our selfish ambitions, and goals that conflict with His goal. Follow Him and in the process become a different kind of person. Jesus did not say: *"Make yourself something and then come and follow me."* He was saying, *"Follow me and I will make you into the kind of person I have destined you to become."* He does not give us blueprints for self-reconstruction, but tells us to just follow Him promising that if we do, He will make us over.

We tear up *our* limited blueprint for our own lives and follow Him without fully seeing the blueprint from which He is working. This call to discipleship is for all believers and not just for a select few. Those who through fear or unwillingness prefer to stay with their own plans for their lives, miss not only the rewards of His kingdom, but the great adventure of following Him and becoming more like Him through the refashioning work of the Holy Spirit.

The kingdom of God is not for the "self made" men, but is found in the hearts and lives of all of those who are genuinely building their lives on the promises of God. Most of the world, consists of that which is built on the power of man rather than the power of God. For this reason we have sometimes been led to believe that involvement with secular activity could never be God's highest and best for any life. However, secular activity can be as blessed as Church activity if that work has its origin in the promises of God more than the prowess of man. *"Unless the Lord builds the house, those who build it labor in vain"* (Psalm 127:1). It is not whether a work is secular or religious that makes it valuable or worthless to God, but whether or not He is the author and the power behind the work.

Coming away from self-dependence and learning to build our whole lives on the grace, power, and person of God brings us into a living experience of the kingdom in all that we do.

CHAPTER 4

THE NEW YOU

We have seen how God made provision for the forgiveness of our sins, enabling us to approach Him and receive His love and grace. God, however, has an even greater purpose for us than this. He has provided the means for us to grow to be more and more like Him.

> God has provided the means for us to grow to be more and more like Him.

God expects all of us who have been adopted into His royal family to yield our conduct and character to be changed to conform to His highest and most wonderful standards. Just as a newborn baby is not a member of his family on the basis of his conduct but on the basis of his inheritance, so, too, we are adopted into the family of God freely, not on the basis of our conduct but on the basis of adoption. However, as time goes by, the parents of the baby are going to expect him to live up to the family standards and to show forth character and behavior similar to that of the parents.

God adopted us into His family when our behavior left much to be desired, but as time goes on He expects us to be able to exhibit more and more of His character and behave in a way that is more and more in keeping with His nature and standards.

But how can we who are fallen human beings, behave with the high standards of our holy God? It was precisely because we were unable to do this that we needed God's

> *God literally offers us a spiritual heart transplant to replace the old failing spirit.*

forgiveness in the first place. If we failed to live up to His standards before we accepted His forgiveness, will we not fail equally now? The answer to this question would be "Yes" if God did no more for us than forgive our sins.

However, He offers us even more than forgiveness. He gives us the gift of a new heart of love to replace the old corrupted selfish heart. He literally offers us a spiritual heart transplant to replace the old failing spirit (heart) that was unable to function with the kind of character which God intends us to have. This new heart which God gives us is the same Spirit (heart) which moved Jesus and empowered Him to live as the perfect Son of God.

The prophets Ezekiel foretold this amazing spiritual heart transplant many years earlier by. *"I will give you a new heart, and a new spirit I will put within you. And I will remove the heart of stone from your flesh and give you a heart of flesh. And I will put my Spirit within you, and cause you to walk in my statutes and be careful to obey my rules."* (Ezekiel 36:26-27)

"Behold the days are coming, says the Lord, when I will make a new covenant with the house of Israel and with the house of Judah, not like the covenant which I made with their fathers when I took them by the hand to bring them out of the land of Egypt, My covenant which they broke, though I was their husband, says the Lord. But this is the covenant which I will make with the house of Israel after those days, says the Lord: I will put my law within them, and I will write it upon their hearts; and I will be their God, and they shall be my people." (Jer. 31:31-34)

Just as it would be unrealistic to expect a man with a severely decayed heart to be able to perform all the activities of a healthy man, it would be unrealistic to expect men with decayed spiritual hearts to behave as men with perfect spiritual hearts. God's answer is to give us the spiritual heart transplant that was prophesied by the prophet Ezekiel and which Jeremiah described as a "New Covenant."

It is only after He has removed our corrupted hearts and replaced them with a new perfect spiritual heart that He expects us to behave as spiritually healthy men and women. In Jesus, God offers every member of the race of Adam a spiritual heart transplant, and it is this new heart that can produce the kind of inner life that will bring forth in all of us the character and behavior God wants us to have.

Jesus put it this way: *"Are grapes gathered from thorns, or figs from thistles? So every sound tree bears good fruit, but the bad tree bears evil fruit. A sound tree cannot bear evil fruit nor can a bad tree bear good fruit. Every tree that does not bear good fruit is cut down and thrown into the fire. Thus you will know them by their fruits"* (Matthew 7:16-20).

The solution to the problem of our bad behavior as human beings is to replace the source of our wrong behavior with a perfect source. Jesus came not to IMPROVE our old natures but to replace them with His own. Everything that is, acts according to its nature. Cats behave like cats, dogs like dogs, giraffes like giraffes and humans like humans. We have inherited, by the ordinary laws of genetics, a nature that is self-orientated and rebellious toward God. This was not the way man was originally made, but it is the way he has become since the primeval fall. That nature is passed on from parent to child.

God's purpose for man however, is that he carry the likeness of God in his nature, character and behavior. Since He can only act according to his nature, God's solution is thoroughly radical. He forgives man of the shortcomings of his old nature, and then replaces the old nature with a nature that is new - the nature of God Himself in human form. As man lives from the new nature, he will show forth the character of God in human form. It will be natural for him to act in a godly way.

On the earth today, there are two distinct species of human beings: those who have the nature of Adam and those who have the nature of God. All men are born "Adamians" (i.e. with the nature of Adam) but on the day God assumed a human nature, there appeared on the earth the first man who had a divine nature in human form.

On the day of the resurrection, this Man began to share His nature with all who would lay down their own Adam natures and receive of His Spirit. *"But to all who received him, who believed in His name, He gave power to become children of God; who were born, not of blood nor of the will of the flesh nor of the will of man, but of God"* (John 1:12-13). Here John is saying that receiving the life of Jesus makes us children of God.

Paul writes about the contrast between the old Adam nature and the new Christ nature in a way that makes clear the radical new beginning provided by this new nature, now available to all of us through Jesus. *"Thus it is written, "The first man Adam became a living being"; the last Adam became a life-giving spirit. But it is not the spiritual which is first but the physical, and then the spiritual. The first man was from the earth, a man of dust; the second man is from heaven. As was the man of dust, so are those who are of the dust; and as is the man of heaven, so are those who are of heaven. Just as we have borne the image of the man of dust, we shall also bear the image of the man of heaven"* (I Cor 15:45-49).

Every living thing behaves according to its nature and reproduces only that which has an identical nature to it. God's solution to the problems of our ungodly nature is to replace it with the divine-human nature which was in Jesus. He lays the axe to the root of our old nature and replaces it with the

> *God's solution to the problems of our ungodly nature is to replace it with the divine-human nature which was in Jesus.*

root system of His own life. *"Even now the axe is laid to the root of the trees; every - tree therefore that does not bear good fruit is cut down and thrown into the fire"* (Matthew 3:10). Jesus gives the illustration to show that He has not come to reform our old natures but to cut them off and to replace them with the nature of His new life.

The real Christian life is not a self-improvement course, though it has often been presented that way. It does not consist in an effort to improve, reform, or rehabilitate our old nature, but consists in a replacement of it by a new nature. As has often been said, it is not a CHANGED life but an EXCHANGED life; not a reformed life but a replaced life, which God gives us to live according to His ways.

The Crow And The Blackbird

Once upon a time there was a very ambitious crow. He wanted to be able to sing beautifully like a blackbird. He did not like the way he sang and he was determined not to remain like the rest of his relatives and ancestors. He was going to become a great singer. He worked very hard, watched his diet carefully, exercised strenuously, studied diligently and practiced daily with all the determination it would take for him to become a great singer.

And so he applied himself to fulfill this great ambition. Years went by, hard years filled with long hours of study, practice and exercise, but in spite of all his effort and willingness, at the end of that time all that would come forth from his crow beak was a raucous "Caw! Caw!" With all of his music study and practice and training, he could not significantly improve upon his singing. Indeed he had studied and read so much about music that he knew more about the subject than any bird alive, including the mellifluous blackbirds who did not even know how to read music. The poor crow was greatly dejected. There never was a more determined bird, and yet it seemed that it was going to take something more than determination or will-power. He was frustrated.

One day as he was reading his morning newspaper, he read there about a famous surgeon who was able to perform the amazing surgical feat of transplanting voices. "This is what I need," he thought. "All my efforts up until now have not succeeded into making my voice sound like that of a blackbird. I will fly to the surgeon and ask him to give me a voice transplant to replace my crow's voice box with a blackbird's. "

So he met with the distinguished surgeon. He was accepted for surgery. When the blackbird voice became available, the crow was operated upon and received a transplant of a blackbird's voice box to replace his own. In due time, after the healing had taken place and the surgical stitches removed, at last the crow could begin to try out his new voice. He began to sing, beautiful sweet notes, just like those of a blackbird. Just as it had been natural for him to sing like a crow before he had the operation, it was now perfectly natural for him to sing like a blackbird.

The new heart, which we receive from Jesus, is a spiritual transplant operation, which replaces our old human heart with the Spirit of Jesus. This transplant is called the new birth. It is as natural for the new heart which Jesus gives us (which is His Spirit) to love as it was for our old heart to look out for its own interests and to be self centered. Jesus

> *The new heart, which we receive from Jesus, is a spiritual transplant operation, which replaces our old human heart with the Spirit of Jesus.*

promised this new heart to those who would receive it. The prophets foresaw it, as we have seen, and finally on the day of the resurrection Jesus made this heart available to His disciples who were commissioned to announce to all men that this heart was available to as many as would receive it.

"Whoever drinks of the water that I shall give him will never thirst; the water that I shall give him will become in him a spring of water welling up to eternal life" (John 4:14).

"If any one thirst, let him come to me and drink. He who believes in me as the scripture has said, "Out of his heart shall flow rivers of living water. "Now this He said about the Spirit, which those who believed in Him were to receive; for as

yet the Spirit had not been given, because Jesus was not yet glorified." (John 7:37-39).

This Spirit Jesus gives us is a replacement for our bankrupt old natures which He bore on the cross. We can receive not only forgiveness for the old as we have seen, but we can also lay it down on Jesus and replace it with the life of His Spirit. This becomes, as He promised, a river of life, righteousness, love and joy welling up within all that receive it. This is what Paul means when he says *"If any one is in Christ, he is a new creation; the old has passed away, Behold the new has come. All this is from God, who through Christ reconciled us to himself and gave us the ministry of reconciliation."* (2 Corinthians 5:17-18)

The Polluting Factory

Here is one more example to illustrate the radical nature of this new life that Jesus gives us.

Once there was a beautiful valley, nestled between the wooded peaks of a great mountain range. How beautiful the valley was, and how unspoiled. One day the head of a large paper company came to the valley and spoke with the people of the valley. He was aware of their economic problems and he wanted to help them. He also wanted to build a factory in the heart of their valley to make paper from wood pulp. At first, the people of the valley welcomed the idea. Their economy desperately needed an industry that would provide employment for the people and so they agreed to allow the factory to be built.

Time went by. A few years after the factory had been in operation, the happiness of the valley people began to change to disappointment and even anger towards the new industrial plant. Since the factory had been in operation, the clear bright air of the valley had been replaced by gray sooty smog. Gone were the pristine scenic views, and on most days one could not even see the nearest mountains because of the sooty pall of smoke.

The county commissioner began to take action. He met with the factory executives and explained to them that the factory was violating their clean air standards. The factory owners pleaded for patience and forgiveness, explaining how difficult it was to operate a factory such as theirs without such waste and still produce a profit. The county officials forgave them; however, there was still no improvement. Again and again the county officials complained to the factory executives and again and again the factory executives pleaded for patience and forgiveness. Again and again the county officials had patience with them and forgave them.

After some years the county officials began to realize that while the act of forgiveness did enable them to coexist with the factory owners and executives, it was doing nothing to remedy the situation. They came up with a costly, but effective solution. They collected money through a special tax and purchased a new smoke free power system for the factory. The old furnaces and chimneys were destroyed and replaced with new pollution-free energy system. Now the offending factory was not just forgiven but changed so that it was no longer an offense. Everybody was very happy.

This is exactly what God has done for us in Christ. He has forgiven the transgressions of our old nature and replaced our offending natures with the nature of His own Son. *"If anyone is in Christ, he is new creation, the old has passed away, behold the new has come."* (2 Cor 5:17)

Under New Management - Jesus As Lord

When we come into union with Jesus, our lives come under new management. Before we were under the control of our own will and mind, as Isaiah says: *"All we like sheep have gone astray, have turned everyone to his own way."* (Isaiah 53:6) Now we are dead to the control of Satan and self as we come under the control of God through Jesus in the Holy Spirit.

In this realm we begin to plan our lives in consultation with Him, learning not to do things any longer in our own misguided selfish way, but in His way. *"As for God His ways are perfect."* (Ps. 18:30)

We are free from sin only insofar as we are free from self and we are free from self insofar as we are in union and obedient to the Holy Spirit. From now on we are to be controlled not so much by rules and ordinances as by the Spirit of love, joy and kindnessthat has come to live within us.

Our freedom from ordinances is not a freedom to go back to a selfish and self directed life but freedom to go on in obedience to the call and directives of Christ. As we obey Him we will do nothing that is contrary to the fruit of the Spirit or to His teachings. As we live in Him, He in us will fulfill His teachings and lead us to express His likeness.

> *Our freedom from ordinances is not a freedom to go back to a selfish and self directed life but freedom to go on in obedience to the call and directives of Christ.*

Coming away from the management of self, we come under the management of Jesus. He will direct us in every detail in our lives. He will direct us to a life of prayer, to a life of service in accordance with His plans. He will show us how to relate to others, how to use our finances in righteous ways, how to conduct our family life, how to use our time and how to live in the abundant life that He has for us.

Once we come to Christ we are not our own. We are drafted into the exciting destiny of God's plan and the special purposes that He has for each of us. As we yield to His unfolding plan. our lives will take us on a very different course from what it would otherwise have taken. The Spirit of Christ will lead us to respond differently to circumstances and situations and to devote ourselves to different interests than before. There will be the loss of one plan and the gaining of a new plan for our lives. Today Jesus is looking for those who will totally abandon themselves to His call plan and ways. Those who do will enter the abundant life that He has promised His followers. *"I am come that you may have life and have it more abundantly."* (John 10:10)

"I beseech thee therefore brethren by the mercies of God, to present your bodies as a living sacrifice, holy and acceptable to God which is your spiritual worship. Do not be conformed to this world but be transformed by the renewal of your mind that you may prove what is the will of God, what is good and acceptable and perfect. (Romans 12:1-2) The true follower of Jesus makes His body and life available to Jesus for Him to use for the

advancement of His purposes. We yield ourselves to God for anything He may want to do through us or with us. This is the way we serve God. He gave up His life for us that He may live it out through us. Join this adventure!

God will shower His greatest blessings on those who yield their all to Him. He does not coerce us to do anything we are not willing to do, but He works in us an inner desire to do that which He wants us to do. In this way there is a wedding of His will and our wills. We delight to do His will and His will becomes our delight. His will and ours become one in spiritual union. Those who yield to this life of abandonment and union will experience His glory. His love, working in us, will overcome our selfishness and fear.

> God will shower His greatest blessings on those who yield their all to Him.

Taking Up Our Cross

So we see that to put our lives under Jesus' leadership involves the cross. He said, *"If any man would come after me, let him deny himself and take up his cross and follow me. For whoever would save his life will lose it; and whoever loses his life for my sake and the gospel's will save it. For what does it profit a*

67

man, to gain the whole world and forfeit his life?" (Mark 8:34-36)

When we become committed followers of Jesus, we begin to live no longer for ourselves but for Him. We seek God's purposes for our lives rather than what we want to do with them. We look out for His interests rather than our own. Sometimes there is conflict between what we want for ourselves and what God wants for us. God's will is best for us in the long run, but we do not always see it that way. When this conflict arises, we are faced with our cross. Jesus took up His cross when He obeyed God even when it resulted in death. We, too, take up our cross when we obey God's will even when it conflicts with our own. This may result in the loss of status with family and friends, the loss of prestige at work or even among religious friends. The result of our obedience, however, will be an increase in the life of the Spirit in us.

It is not always easy to serve the Lord and to love others. The demands of this love and service may cost us the loss of not only time, personal comfort and status but may even involve physical death. When Jesus asks us to take up our cross and follow Him, He is not asking us to get ourselves executed by crucifixion but to obey God even when it involves loss and is not convenient. The work of God advances in the world today not primarily on the wings of church services, eloquent preaching or religious programs but through lives that have embraced this dimension of the cross. As a tank advances on its caterpillar tracks, so the work of God advances on the tracks of lives that are laid down for him and others in love. - This is true Christianity without Religion!

The cross is not something we are *compelled* to choose. It is something we may or may not choose. Each day there are choices between our convenience and an act of love towards another, between the service of self or the service of God. The choice is always ours: to take up *OUR* cross for the sake of Jesus that others may live, or to choose to live for self, which ends in death. *"...For if you live according to the flesh you will die, but if by the Spirit you put to death the deeds of the body you will live."* (Romans 8:13)

There are then, from what we have seen, three dimensions of the cross in the life of the believer.

- Jesus' death for us whereby He took our sins and gave us right standing with God (See Chapter 1)
- Our legal death with Jesus on His cross whereby our Adam sinful nature died, was buried in the tomb of Jesus (Romans 6:6) and is replaced with the new nature of Jesus (See Chapter 4)

- Our own cross (Mark 8:34) is experienced when we live to obey God surrendering our lives to Him.

The benefits of Jesus' cross are appropriated by faith. The benefits of our own cross are enjoyed through obedience. Faith in the cross of Jesus produces the salvation of our spirits. Obedience to the Spirit causes us to experience our cross and results in the progressive salvation of our souls . Will you choose to take up your cross each day for Jesus?

As we embark on the life of obedience we do not win our salvation but we allow the life and love of Christ to come into ever increasing manifestation through us.

CHAPTER 5

LIFE AND POWER

J esus came that we *"might have life and have it more abundantly"* (John 10:10) He came, as we have seen, to be our Passover Lamb to die for our sins, taking the blame, the shame and the condemnation we deserved. He also came to give us NEW LIFE - His Resurrection Life. The life born in Bethlehem had to die, but the Resurrection Life never dies. What is born of the flesh can die, but what we receive when we are born again is Resurrection Life, which lives forever.

This new life comes to us in the Person of the Holy Spirit. He is the Resurrection Life that Jesus gives. Jesus referred to the Holy Spirit as "the promise of the Father." He gives the Holy Spirit in two distinct and different ways:

- Firstly, to come to indwell us as the new SOURCE of inner life

- Secondly, to come upon us as the Enabler and Anointing who equips us to participate in the powerful ministry of Jesus.

The first part of the gift of the Holy Spirit gives us a share in the *nature* of Jesus The second part of the gift gives us a share in the *ministry* of Jesus.

The Holy Spirit Within

When Jesus rose from the dead He appeared to His followers and breathed upon them and gave them the gift of the Holy Spirit to dwell **within** them. *"On the evening of that day, the first day of the week, the doors being shut where the disciples were, for fear of the Jews, Jesus came and stood among them and said to them, "Peace be with you". When He had said this He showed them His hands and His side. Then the disciples were glad when they saw the Lord. Jesus said to them again, "Peace be with you. As the Father sent me, even so I send you." And when He had said this, He breathed on them and said to them, "Receive the Holy Spirit. If you forgive the sins of any they are forgiven; if you retain the sins of any they are retained.""* (John 20:19-23)

This breathing by Jesus on His disciples reminds us of the moment when God created man from the dust of the earth. He breathed on it and formed man from it. (Genesis 2:7) Now

Jesus breathes a new life into earthly man - a life that Adam never had before the fall. This life that Jesus imparts is a share in His own Resurrection Life. He gives it to all who receive it by faith and who by faith lay down their Adam Life (and all its inheritance received at natural birth) in the tomb of Jesus. *"But as many as received Him, to them He gave the right to become children of God, to those who believe in His name: who were born not of blood, nor of the will of the flesh, nor of the will of man, but of God."* (John 1:12-13)

The Spirit that was present in Jesus and raised Him from the dead then comes *into* us to make us spiritually alive and energizes our lives. *"The Spirit; who raised Jesus from the dead will give life to your mortal bodies through His Spirit which dwells in you."* (Romans 8:11) *The first man, Adam, became a living soul, the last Adam Jesus became a life giving spirit"* (1 Cor. 15:45)

> *As we put our faith in this the Holy Spirit pours God's love into our hearts and we receive the Spirit of adoption and sonship*

When Jesus breathed on His disciples on that great day, they received into their innermost beings, the very life that was in Him. This life was to be the motivating and driving force of their lives forever. Until this time man was controlled by his soul (his mind, intellect will and emotions). Now the living Spirit and Life of God Himself could motivate him. *"He who is united with the Lord becomes one Spirit with Him. "* (I Cor. 6: 17)

Through the Atoning Sacrifice of Jesus the barrier, which sin had made between man and God's love is broken down. As we put our faith in this the Holy Spirit pours God's love into our hearts and we receive the Spirit of adoption and sonship. *"Therefore, having been justified by faith, we have peace with God through our Lord Jesus Christ, through whom also we have access by faith into this grace in which we stand and rejoice in the hope of the glory of God... Now hope does not disappoint because God's love is poured into our hearts by the Holy Spirit who was given to us. "* (Romans 5:1-2 & 5) Through the Holy Spirit we actually experience the love of God coming into our hearts.

The Second Gift Of The Holy Spirit

After His followers had received this New Life from Jesus, He remained with them for forty days. (Mark 16:19) Finally, the day came when Jesus was to depart from the earth, at least in the visible sense. The time had now come for the disciples to go into every corner of the earth to proclaim the reconciliation that God had accomplished through Jesus, and to invite all men to receive for themselves the "new engine" of the Holy Spirit (the Resurrection Life of Jesus). To perform this task would not only take courage, boldness, and great love but the powerful presence of God Himself.

Jesus had promised, however to send the Holy Spirit to them in a new way, to come *upon* them to guide and equip them. His presence with them would confirm their message with healings, signs and wonders. As He was departing, He said to them: *"And behold, I send the promise of the Father upon you: but stay in the city until you are clothed with power from on high."* (Lk. 24:29) *"But you shall receive power when the Holy Spirit has come upon you; and you shall be my witnesses in Jerusalem, and in all Judea, and Samaria and to the end of the earth."* (Acts 1: 8)

Jesus tells His disciples to wait in Jerusalem until the Holy Spirit would come *upon* them. On the day of Jesus' resurrection they had already received the Holy Spirit to come *within* them (Jn. 20:21-22). Now the Holy Spirit was to come *upon* them to empower them, to do the works that Jesus had called them to do. On the day of Pentecost, the Holy Spirit did come *upon* them in a spectacular way, and from that moment they were empowered to proclaim the gospel in love and strength. They were launched on a life that would be lived out in the obedient pattern of Jesus.

Just as Jesus Himself was filled with the Holy Spirit for thirty years before the Holy Spirit came ***upon*** Him, the disciples were filled with the Holy Spirit for more than forty days before the Holy Spirit came ***upon*** them to anoint them for their mission. Today all believers receive the Holy Spirit when they put their faith in Jesus, and ask Him to live in their hearts. However many neglect to ask Jesus to anoint them with the power of the Holy Spirit to equip them for their calling and to continue His works on earth.

The Baptism in the Holy Spirit that Jesus gave to the one hundred and twenty (male and female) disciples on the day of Pentecost is a gift He offers to believers of all times who sincerely ask. *"For the promise is to you and to your children and to all who are afar off as many as the Lord our God will call."(*Acts 2:39) He offers this great gift. It is not automatic however; we must offer ourselves to Him and ask Him to give us the Holy Spirit. *"Which of you if he would ask his father for bread would receive a stone, or ask his father for an egg would receive stone. If you being evil know how to give your children good gifts how much more will the heavenly father give the Holy Spirit to those who ask."* Jesus will not force the anointing of the Holy Spirit on any of us. We must ask Him to empower us with His Spirit to do His works.

New Birth & Baptism In The Spirit

The New Birth is a *"drink of living water."* We receive it when we ask Jesus to live by His Spirit in our hearts. The Holy Spirit then comes *into* us. This is the new birth. When we are BAPTIZED with the Holy Spirit, the Holy Spirit comes UPON us to anoint us to be effective and powerful witnesses for Christ and His Kingdom. (When we drink a glass of water, we get wet on the *inside*, but remain dry *outside*.) When we get baptized in water, on the other hand, we remain dry on the *inside* but get wet on the *outside*. Obviously, the two are not the same. A drink is not a baptism. So, too, the "drink" of the Spirit of God (new birth) and the "baptism" (anointing) with the Spirit of God are two distinct realities.

The Holy Spirit comes INTO us when Jesus gives us a drink of living water. When Jesus *baptizes* us with the Holy Spirit, He causes us to be surrounded with the presence and power of the Holy Spirit who comes UPON us through this Baptism. It is not hard for anyone to see that there is an enormous difference between a DRINK and an IMMERSION or baptism. Jesus gives us first a *drink* of His Spirit and then an *immersion into that Spirit.*

In Old Testament days, no one had yet received the Holy Spirit WITHIN them. However, in those days the Holy Spirit was very active and came UPON the prophets, priests and kings to equip them for their offices. In those days, the Holy Spirit came UPON people to anoint them for a task but could not come WITHIN any of them. That is why John says talking about the period before Jesus' death and resurrection: *"as yet the Spirit had not been given because Jesus was not yet glorified."* (John 7:39) He writes, *"On the last day of the feast, the great day, Jesus stood up and proclaimed: "If any man thirst let him come to me and drink. He who believes in me, as the scripture has said, out of his heart shall flow rivers of living water." Now this He said about the Spirit which those who believed in Him were to receive; for as yet the Spirit had not been given because Jesus was not yet glorified."* (John 7:37)

The Holy Spirit could not be given to come WITHIN us as a new principle of life until after Jesus' death and resurrection. Jesus first had to bear our old fallen Adam natures to the cross before they could be replaced by the new nature of His Resurrection Life. As we have seen, it was those who had drunk of the Spirit on the day of Jesus' resurrection who went to "The Upper Room" to await the Baptism with the Holy Spirit, which they received on the day of Pentecost.

Jesus offers New Life to all who believe in Him. If we accept what He offers, admit the inadequacy of our Adam nature, and lay them down, we can receive the Holy Spirit WITHIN us and be Born Again. Then we are also offered a share in Jesus' Anointing through the Baptism in the Holy Spirit.

Believers first receive first receive the Spirit WITHIN as the replacement for their sinful self-life, and then they can present themselves to receive the Baptism with the Holy Spirit - the Spirit UPON them. (We receive both by faith once we ask and admit our need.)

So we see that Jesus gives the Holy Spirit to all who will receive Him in two distinct ways:

- Firstly, as the LIFE of the Holy Spirit to be a river of pure water flowing from within our innermost beings; and
- Secondly, as the supernatural Equipper and Presence who enables us to be bold Christian witnesses and obedient servants.

The first is the Resurrection gift of the Holy Spirit, and the second is the Pentecost gift of the Holy Spirit. The first giving of the Holy Spirit reproduces the character of Christ in us, (the fruit of the Spirit) and the second empowers us to share in the ministry of Jesus and to proclaim the gospel in power. In some instances the giving of the Holy Spirit *within* and *upon* can happen simultaneously.

The Gift Of Tongues

Most of the things of the Spirit are beyond the reach of our minds. The Holy Spirit also enables us to pray (if we cooperate with Him) in a language that reaches beyond the limits of our minds. *"Likewise the Spirit helps us in our weaknesses; for we do not know how to pray as we on ought but the. Spirit himself intercedes for us with sighs too deep for words. And He who searches the hearts of men knows what is the mind of the Spirit, because the Spirit intercedes for the saints according to the will of God."* (Romans 8:26-27)

The gift of tongues and various other manifestations of the Spirit (including prophecy, interpretation of tongues, the word of wisdom, the word of knowledge, faith, healing, miracles and discernment of spirits) can evidence themselves in the lives of believers who ask Jesus to anoint them with His Spirit. Those who actively receive the Holy Spirit can willingly pray in tongues as the Spirit gives them the ability. *We* do the praying and the Holy Spirit makes it a language of deep communication to God. It is not automatic. The person must begin to speak words in a language he does not understand, and the Holy Spirit makes it a language that is understood by God. In this way we are enabled to pray in a way that is deeper than our understanding.

On the day of Pentecost *"they were all filled with the Holy Spirit and began to SPEAK in other tongues, as the spirit gave them utterance."* (Acts 2:4). ***They*** did the speaking and the Holy Spirit gave them utterance. When we speak in our own language, we use our tongues and our vocal chords. To speak in tongues, we do the same, except we remove the censorship of the mind to be subject to the Spirit. It is not magic - it is partnership. *"For one who speaks in a tongue, speaks not to men but to God; for no one understands him but he utters mysteries in the Spirit. On the other hand, he who prophesies speaks to men for their upbuilding, encouragement and consolation. He who speaks in a tongue edifies himself, but he who prophesies edifies the church. Now I want you all to speak in tongues but even more prophesy."* (1 Cor. 14:2)

Have you received both aspects of Jesus' gift of the Holy Spirit, the drink of living water to fill your heart with the life of Jesus and the pouring out of the Holy Spirit to anoint you to the service and the self-emptying of Jesus?

The empowerment of the Holy Spirit is given only to those who are aware of their abject inability to live the righteous life and do the works of Jesus apart from His help. Jesus said to Paul: *"My grace is sufficient for you, for my strength is made perfect in weakness."* (2 Cor.

12:9) Paul therefore could say: *"I will all the more gladly boast of my weakness, that the power of God may rest upon me for when I am weak then I am strong."* (2 Cor. 12:9) When we are most aware of our weakness and inadequacy, we can best draw by faith from the strength of God and receive the help of the Holy Spirit.

A Prayer To Receive The Holy Spirit

Jesus, I thank you for bearing my sins on your self. I acknowledge that I am a sinner and need you to pay for my guilt. I lay down and turn away from my sins and lay down my selfish Adam life so that You can come to live in my heart. I believe that You have made atonement for my sins by dying on the cross in my place and rising from the dead. Jesus, I ask you to come to me, live in my heart, and love through my heart. I receive that "drink of living water" – the Holy Spirit. I now present my life to You and I ask You to enable me to live in accordance with Your ways of love and according to your Word. Through You God is my Father and I am a new creation and a forgiven and blessed child of God. I come out from the dominion of darkness and place myself under your protection and leadership, and I ask You to be the Managing Director and Lord of the rest of my life. Amen.

A Prayer To Receive Baptism In The Spirit

Dear Jesus, I give myself to You for Your purposes. I want my life to be used by You, but I do not have the full power for this so I ask you now to baptize me (mightily) with the Holy Spirit and with power. Holy Spirit come upon me with all your gifts and graces. Give me a spirit of love and compassion, power and might, boldness and utterance, faith and humility, revelation and understanding. I receive you now from the hands of Jesus as my Enabler to do the works of a disciple and to live a life dedicated to You and to Your kingdom, and I will pray in tongues (right now) as you give me the ability.

(Pray this prayer in an attitude of receptivity only if you have made a complete consecration of your life to the Lord.)

CHAPTER 7

FREE TO SOAR

"There is therefore now no condemnation for those who are in Christ Jesus. For the law of the spirit of life in Christ Jesus has set me free from the law of sin and death. For God has done what the law, weakened by the flesh, could not do. Sending His own Son in the likeness of sinful flesh and for sin, He condemned sin in the flesh, in order that the just requirement of the law might be fulfilled in us who walk not according to the flesh but according to the Spirit" (Romans 8:1-4). The work of Jesus on the cross frees us from the penalty of sin, from guilt, condemnation, slavery to sin, selfishness and from the law.

In Romans Chapters six, seven and eight Paul explains that, when we choose to live in the Spirit, we are set free from the power of sin and the Law. Christians often misunderstand this truth. We wonder how God could set us free from the law of Moses with its rules and regulations. We think that it would be dangerous to teach people that when they come into Christ, they are truly free from the law. We fear that if this were preached, people would live lax lives. For this reason, many prefer to teach that we must still keep new and old laws to maintain a right standing with God.

While scarcely any believer will teach that we must keep the whole law that God gave to Moses, many teach that we must keep a modified version of the Mosaic law as interpreted by their particular denomination.

In the first two verses of Romans 8 (quoted above) there are three laws referred to:

- the law of the Spirit of life
- second, the law of sin and death
- and third, the law of Moses.

"The law of the Spirit of life in Christ Jesus has set me free from the law of sin and death." (Romans 8:2). No religious law given to restrain our sinfulness can ever accomplish what the "*law of the spirit of life*" can do in believers' lives.

Since the time of Adam all men have been subject to "*the law of sin and death*". This law pulls at everyone of us to drag us toward destruction. This law even pulls at born-again believers. However, the Spirit they have received within them is stronger than that negative force of sin and death. The *"law of sin and death"* is like the law of gravity, which holds every one of us down to the earth. The only way for us to escape the earth's gravitational pull is by putting into operation other laws, which are stronger and more powerful than the law of gravity.

We now know that there are indeed laws, which are stronger than the law of gravity. These are the laws of aerodynamics. When an airplane takes off from a runway, it escapes the law of gravity by harnessing the laws of aerodynamics. The law of gravity is still there but as long as the jet engines are engaging the laws of aerodynamics, the airplane is able to fly free from the pull of gravity.

This parallels what God does for us when He places the Resurrection Life of Jesus – the Holy Spirit within us. This is like the law of aerodynamics, which enables the airplane to escape the law of gravity. As long as the engines are running the airplane will remain free from the law of gravity. However, if they are turned off, then, of course, the airplane will fall. As long as we remain in tune with the Resurrection Life of Christ in us, we remain free from the law of sin and death; but if we let go of our union with Christ, we will fall back under the control of sin.

Until the laws of aerodynamics were discovered and we learned to build machines that could harness these laws, it was impossible for man to fly. In a similar way, it was impossible for man to get free from *"the law of sin and death"* until Jesus gave His life to dwell within us. Until then the law that God gave to Moses for the people of Israel *restrained* them, but it did not *free* them from the law of sin and death. It has no power to set anyone free from that law of sin. *"The law was our custodian until Christ came."* (Gal 3:23)

The Holy Spirit is the only antidote to sin. His presence in us is the only power that can lift us free from sin's dominion. Neither religion nor will-power can free us from the power of sin. The gift of the Spirit is God's answer to the sin of the world. The New Covenant is not only a message of forgiveness for past failure - it is also the empowerment by the Spirit to live in love and free from the power of sin. This is the great revolution of the gospel.

An Illustration

The launching of the Space Shuttle from the Kennedy Space Center in Florida, is now a familiar sight. Several days before the launch, the spacecraft is taken out and set in position for launching. The shuttle is secured to the vertical platform by means of several struts and fasteners that hold the shuttle in place. Should they be removed before the rocket engines are fired, the shuttle would be in danger of falling over, knocked down by the wind or pulled down by the force of gravity.

The space shuttle has a destiny to fulfill to get free from the force of gravity's power, which could pull it to the ground. In the days before the launch, the spacecraft stands clumsily, prevented from the destructive power of gravity only by the launching platform to which it is secured. It needs those securing struts to avoid being toppled over and shattered on the ground.

Finally, the day of the launch arrives. The countdown is almost complete and the rockets are ignited. A tremendous surge of power is released within the engines of the launching rockets and the spacecraft begins to rise in a great explosion of power headed to its destination in the heavens. As it rises, it separates from the launching platform and rises above the gravitational pull of the earth. After the rocket engines are ignited, the security struts will be a hindrance to the launching of the rocket if the spacecraft remains secured to them. What has previously been an aid to the spacecraft in its "struggle" against gravity will now be a hindrance to it.

This illustration shows how those who accept the life of Jesus as the driving force of their lives and commit to live by the principles of Jesus' teaching have a new relationship with the law given to Moses and similar religious restraining laws. Religious laws are directed at restraining sin. The life of the Spirit and the teachings of Jesus are for His disciples to direct them in law of love. Just as the launching pad and the bolts were the first stage in the spacecraft's efforts to get free of the law of gravity, so the Law of Moses, and religious laws, are important first steps in restraining us from the law of sin and death. Paul says, *"Now before faith came, we were confined under the law, kept under restraint until faith should be revealed. So that the law was our custodian until Christ came that we might be justified by faith. But now that faith has come, we are no longer under a custodian"* (Gal 3:23-25).

Countless Jewish people in the time of the first apostles, and in every subsequent generation, have seen these truths and have entered into a true and full appropriation of the essence of their Jewish heritage. They see that the Law of Moses was a preparation period for the day of the Messiah and the day when God would write His law within the hearts of all who would come to Him. However, in every generation since Christ, many believers have tried to hold on to the Mosaic Law (or a modified form of it) and still follow Jesus the Messiah.

The scriptures forbid anyone from adding or subtracting from the words of the law. Jesus Himself was most adamant on this point: *"For truly, I say unto you, till heaven and earth pass away not an iota, not a dot will pass from the law until all is accomplished."* (Matthew 5:18) Jesus did not come to destroy the law, but to fulfill it. He brings us into a higher realm of righteousness than that which could be attained through the law. *"For I tell you, unless your righteousness exceeds that of the scribes and Pharisees, you will never enter into the kingdom of heaven"* (Matthew 5:20).

To return to our illustration, the spacecraft will never get into the heavens unless it goes higher and farther than the supports on the launching platform would permit. To get free to go with its powerful rocket engines, it must leave the props at the launching pad. The Shuttle does not destroy the launching pad. It simply rises above it fulfilling its intended purpose. The shuttle leaves the bolts intact, but leaves them behind as it becomes subject to a different law.

Illustration II - The Greasy Pole

The following is another way we can clarify our relationship to *"the law of the Spirit of life in Christ Jesus"*, *"the law of sin and death"* and the law of Moses mentioned in Romans 8:2. The illustration is perhaps a little far-fetched but the point it makes is vitally important.

Imagine a man who tried to get free of the pull of gravity by trying to climb a tall, greasy pole. It was a tremendous struggle for him to keep from slipping. Indeed, he found that the faster he climbed, the more he slipped. The pole did prevent him from falling into the mud beneath, but he was not able to make any upward progress.

After some time, someone came by and attached a great helium balloon to his shoulders. As soon as the balloon was attached, he was now able to let go of the pole without risk of falling into the mud beneath. However, the man was afraid to let go of the pole because he was not quite sure that the balloon would hold him up. Before the balloon had been attached, the pole was the only thing that stood between him and the mud. It had been his only means of escape; thus, it was difficult as he continued to clutch on to that pole, the balloon could not lift him. The pole, which had been a help to him in his effort to get clear of the mud, was now holding him back. Before the balloon was attached, it would have been disastrous to let go of the pole; however now that the balloon was connected to him, the pole ceased to help and had become instead a hindrance to his progress.

Some distance away stood an observer. He had watched the desperate strugglings of the man on the pole. He watched when the balloon had been fixed to the man's shoulders. He watched the man continue to clutch on to the pole fearful of letting go. The observer took a gun from his pocket, aimed in the direction of the man on the pole and shot. The bullet hit the man killing him instantly. Falling dead, the man released his grip on the pole. However, he did not fall to the ground. As he slumped dead, the balloon carried him up and away into the skies.

This tale illustrates some important truths concerning our relationship with the *"law of sin and death"* (which in the story corresponds to the law of gravity), the law of Moses and the laws of religious traditions and ordinances (which are represented by the pole), and the *"law of the Spirit of life in Christ Jesus"* (represented by the balloon). Both the pole and the balloon are used to keep the man free from the mud towards which he is being pulled by the law of gravity. However the pole does not have sufficient power to protect him from the pull of gravity. Even when the balloon was attached, it was not able to lift him until his hands let go of the pole. In a similar way, when the Resurrection Life of Jesus comes into us and we flow with it, we have within us a new principle of incorruptible life which is greater than the pull of sin and death. However, if we are still trying to

> *If we are still trying to escape sin by means of keeping laws, rules and regulations, the life of Jesus cannot carry us.*

escape sin by means of keeping laws, rules and regulations, and religious observances the life of Jesus cannot carry us.

Paul explains that if, after the life of Christ has come into us, we go back to relying on the law (religious observance) Christ will be of no avail to us. Just as the balloon cannot carry us as long as we clutch on to the pole, so Christ cannot carry us as long as we remain attached to the law as our means of spiritual progress. *"You are severed from Christ,"* he writes, *"you who would be justified by the law; you have fallen away from grace."* (Gal. 5:4)

The believers in Galatia, many of whom were Jewish, experienced tremendous blessings and miracles when they were first converted. Later they lost that early sense of blessing, and the demonstration of God's presence among them disappeared. Paul attributed their loss of blessing to their attempt to hold on to the Law of Moses and to Christ at the same time. To keep holding on to the old Law while they tried to follow Christ, neutralized their connection with Christ. They were still attached to Christ, but they had bound up His presence in them. *"If justification were through the law, then Christ died to no purpose."* he writes (Gal 2:21)

As mentioned, Jesus said, He came not to destroy the Law but to fulfill it *"Think not that I am come to destroy the law or the prophets: I am not come to destroy, but to fulfill."* (Mt 5:17) In the Sermon on the Mount, He shows that the Law must be fulfilled by the inner work of the Spirit creating a deeper righteousness than the external Laws of Sinai. His deeper righteousness comes from within and can only be fulfilled as His Spirit is placed within us as a fountain of deeper righteousness.

The negative experience of those Galatian Christians has been repeated in the lives of thousands of believers. Beginning with simple faith in the mercy of God, they experience His blessings and goodness. Then they seek to maintain their union with God through laws instead of through simple, ongoing dependence on Christ and they lose their blessing.

God's Promises Not Changed

Through the years Christians have often abused this revelation of the changed relationship we have with the Law of Moses (when we come to faith in Christ and receive the Holy Spirit) to justify anti-Jewish and anti-Semitic teaching. By pointing out the shortcoming of the Law, Jesus, Paul and the other apostles were not putting down Judaism – they were pointing out the inadequacy of ANY religion (Jewish or Christian or any other) to establish our relationship with God. No law (system of religious ritual and moral observance) can establish our relationship with God or set us free from sin's dominion – only faith in the Atoning sacrifice and the infilling of the Spirit of God can do this.

God's unique purpose for the Jewish people is unchanged by the bringing in of permanent Atonement and the giving of the Holy Spirit. God called the family of Abraham, Isaac and Jacob over four hundred years before the Law was givenThat call exists for all generations, even when the Law is becoming obsolete. The covenant and call on Israel supersedes and precedes the law that was given through Moses. The New Testament says *"the gifts and call of God* (on the people of Israel*) are irrevocable."* (Rom. 11: 29)

"In speaking of a New Covenant He treats the first as obsolete. And what is becoming obsolete and growing old is ready to vanish away." (He. 8:13) When we say, as Hebrews says, that the Law is becoming obsolete, we are not saying that God's covenant with and call on the Jewish people is obsolete. We are saying that relying on Jewish, or any religious observance, is obsolete when we rely on the cleansing power of the Blood of Jesus and the empowerment of the Holy Spirit.

Note that the Bible does not say that the first law *is* obsolete but that it is ***becoming*** obsolete. The Law is still needed to show us our sinfulness. It is becoming obsolete as more and more people put their faith in the work of Jesus and receive the Holy Spirit, and as we rely less and less on the external restraints of the Law and religion and more and more on the inner life of the Spirit.

Empowered For A New Way of Living

Jesus does not set aside the Law but demonstrated its uselessness to make us righteous. Neither the Law nor any religious ritual or regimen can reconcile us to God nor liberate us from sin - only the work of God in the Atoning sacrifice can do that.

Some believers have the mistaken idea that the life of Christ is given to enable us to *keep* the law. This is a mistaken impression. The early Christians, even those who were Jewish, did not keep the Law all of the time. *"If you, though a Jew, live like a Gentile and not like a Jew, how can you compel the Gentiles to live like Jews?"* Paul wrote in his letter to the Galatians (Galatians 2:14). He was pointing out that Peter, one of the greatest Jewish leaders of the church, did not consistently obey the Law. The early believers sometimes observed the Law and other religious

> *The first law is becoming obsolete as we rely less and less on the external restraints of the law and more and more on the inner life the Spirit.*

customs of their culture but they no longer ***relied*** on these to establish their relationship with God. *"The law was our custodian until Christ came that we might be justified by faith. But now that faith has come, we are no longer under a custodian; for in Christ Jesus you are all sons of God through faith."* (Galatians 3:24-26).

The law has not changed, nor can it ever be changed, but we have been taken away from its custody. Through Moses, God placed the Jewish people under the custody of the law, but in Jesus, He wants to remove them from the law and to place them under *"the law of the Spirit of life in Christ Jesus"*. John writes, *"For the law was given through Moses, grace and truth came through Jesus Christ."* (John 1:17).

Just as the man on the pole could make no more progress, after the balloon was attached, until he let go of the pole to go with the balloon, so today many believers cannot progress in the Spirit until they put obedience to the leading of the Holy Spirit and the teachings of Jesus above every other law in their lives. We cannot go on to maturity if we are relying on religious observance rather than the life of the Holy Spirit.

God is calling His people to maturity, but we cannot move on towards that maturity as long as we substitute the leading of the law for the leading of the Holy Spirit. *"On the one hand, a former commandment is set aside because of its weakness and uselessness (for the law made nothing perfect); on the other hand, a better hope is introduced, through which we draw near to God "* (Hebrews 7:18-19).

The Law has a purpose in God's dealing with us. It shows us our sin and our need of redemption but it can never set us free. Jesus has brought in a whole new order of reality in our relationship with God. By His sacrifice, He has also brought in a new and eternal priesthood in which He is both eternal priest and eternal sacrifice.

Hebrews points out that *"When there is a change of priesthood, there is necessarily a change in the law as well."* (Hebrew 7:12). Jesus' death fulfills the requirements of the old law and inaugurates a new law - the law of the spirit of life in Christ Jesus! If believers are to put their faith in the eternal priestly work of Jesus, then they must come under His new law which exceeds the old law.

"But as it is, Christ has obtained a ministry which is more excellent than the old just as the covenant He mediates is better, since it is enacted on better promises. For if the first covenant had been faultless, there would have been no occasion for a second. "He finds fault with them when He says: "The days will come, says the Lord, when I will establish a new covenant with the house of Israel and the house

of Judah... In speaking of a new covenant He treats the first as obsolete. And what is becoming obsolete and growing old is ready to vanish away."" (Hebrews 8:6-8,13). Many believers are afraid to let go of that which is obsolete.

Legalism, License & Liberty

The life of the Spirit is not legalism nor license but liberty. Those who rely on religion are under legalism and can never enter the life of the Spirit. Those who ignore God's moral standards fall into the bondage and power of sin. But those who lean on the Holy Spirit experience the glorious liberty of the children of God – freedom from condemnation, freedom from guilt and freedom from sin.

In saying that we have been released from the Law of Moses we do *not* say that we have been released from obedience to God. Some believers have mistakenly understood their freedom from the old law as a freedom from *all* law. This, of course, is not the case. There is only one thing that can free us from the *law* of sin and death, and that is "*the law of the spirit of life in Christ Jesus*" (Romans 8:2*)*. A new law has come to replace the old law. This new law is the law of the life of Christ Jesus in us – the "law of the spirit of life."

This new life does not empower us to keep the old Law. We are discharged form our guilt under the Law and empowered by the Spirit to keep and fulfill the new law. *"A new commandment I give to you that you love one another as I have loved you."* (John 13:34) This new law is not a written code but a law, a life of selfless love which is infused into us by the Holy Spirit. The believers' responsibility is to remain attuned to the love, kindness and selflessness which this life of the Spirit causes to arise within the heart of every Christian. Just as the man attached to the balloon would fall instantly if he let go of the balloon, so we who cleave to Christ are freed from the restraints of religion only as we cleave to Him and do only those things, which are in harmony with His Word, His ways, and the New Life He has infused into us.

Married To Another

The move from obedience to external law to obedience to Christ can be compared to a wedding. On the day of her wedding the bride moves from her father's care to her husband's care. During her childhood and adolescence she was in the care of her father and owed him her obedience. On her wedding day she moves away from her dependency on her father and is released from any obedience to him. From now on she will work out her life in relationship with her husband. She will, of course, always honor and respect her father, but she is no longer required to give him her obedience. In fact, it would be quite damaging to her relationship with her husband if she sought to obey her father as well as her husband. When she married, she was expected to leave her father and mother and to cleave to her husband.

In a similar way, when a person enters into union with Christ, he must leave the Law (as good and wonderful as it is) and cleave to Him. If this does not take place, the union will never become strong. This does not mean that Jewish believers in Christ should leave behind their Jewish culture or their Jewishness, but they should lay aside any adherence to the Law and traditions as their means of getting and staying close to God and as their principle of guidance.

In this discussion of the Christian's relationship with the Law, no criticism of the law is intended, no more than the bride's departure from her parents to unite with her husband would constitute a criticism of them. Obedience to her parents has prepared her for her new life with her husband.

In a similar way the Jewish people's relationship with the Law was intended as a temporary arrangement to prepare them for obedience to Christ through His implanted Spirit. The religious laws which many of us have grown up with in church can have a similar purpose in our lives inasmuch as they prepare us for obedience to Christ in the Spirit, but they can be counter productive after we have been 'born-again' and filled with the Spirit of God.

In Romans, Chapter 7, Paul explains that we have been freed from the law so that we can follow Jesus. He compares it to a woman being released from a difficult marriage so that she can marry the man of her heart. Under the law, there is no way out of this marriage except by the death of one of the spouses. The only way out for this unhappy lady is for her husband to die or for her to die. Paul goes on to explain that since we died in Christ, we have been discharged from the law because the law is binding on a person only during his life. *"Likewise, my brethren, you have died to the law through the Body of Christ so that you may belong to another, to him who has been raised from the dead in order that we may bear fruit for God. ... But now we are DISCHARGED FROM THE LAW, dead to that which held us captive so that we serve not under the old written code but in the new life of the Spirit."* (Romans 7:4, 6)

Believers have died in Christ and can begin a brand new life through His Spirit. Being freed from the law and discharged from its obligations, we are free to be led by the loving Spirit of Jesus our Messiah. Only through death can we be discharged from the old law. Since we died in Christ, we have been released from the law which was been given to govern and restrain the natural life we received from our father Adam. When we come to Christ, we lay down that life at the cross of Jesus and accept the new life of the Spirit.

Jesus' life is for those who have come to an end of the efforts of self-justification of the Adamic man and for those who have repented of working in their old energies and released themselves to work in and respond to the new life of the Spirit. The balloon in our illustration could only carry the man after he had ceased his own efforts to escape the pull of gravity. After he had died, the balloon had no resistance and could carry him easily. We should be dead to the stirrings and strugglings of our own desperate efforts and alive to the promptings and leading of the Spirit of life in us. *"So you also must consider yourselves dead to sin and ALIVE to God in Christ Jesus"* (Romans 6:11). When He died we died! Now it remains for us to consider ourselves dead to sin each day when sin comes knocking on our door.

Jesus explained the truths we have been explaining here to His disciples in a different way when He took Peter, James and John with Him for prayer on Mount Tabor. *"And behold there appeared to them Moses and Elijah talking with him. And Peter said to Jesus: "Lord, it is well that we are here; if you wish, I will make*

three booths here, one for you and one for Moses
and one for Elijah." He was still speaking when,
lo, a bright cloud overshadowed them, and a
voice from the cloud said, "This is my beloved
Son with whom I am well pleased; listen to him."
When the disciples heard this, they fell on their
faces, and were filled with awe. But Jesus came
and touched them, saying, "Rise, and have no
fear." And when they lifted up their eyes, **they
saw no one but Jesus only**. And as they were
coming down the mountain Jesus said to them
"Tell no one the vision, until the Son of man is
raised from the dead."" (Matthew 17:3-9)

When Peter saw Moses and Elijah talking
together with Jesus, he was pleased that Jesus
was in such illustrious company and wanted to
build a booth for each of them. The voice of God
was heard commanding them to hear and obey
Jesus and when they looked up again, they saw
only Jesus. Peter wanted to have Jesus with
Moses and Elijah. Moses and Elijah represent the

law and the prophets
and Peter's desire to
build a booth for each
symbolizes his desire
to have Jesus **and** the
law. The fact that Moses and Elijah faded and
God's voice commanded obedience to Jesus
indicates that Moses and Elijah were receding to
give precedence to Jesus.

*Jesus brings us from
outer observance to
inner obedience.*

Jesus commanded them not to report the vision until after the resurrection because the hour of discharge from the Law of Moses was not until Jesus had paid the penalty for all of our transgressions under the law. By dying for us, He included us in His death so that we could be "discharged from the Law" to receive the new life of the Spirit and obey Jesus. Moses and Elijah had fulfilled their mission and now the kingdom of God was at hand.

In this realm it is the new "law of the spirit of life in Christ Jesus" working together with the commands of Jesus that must be obeyed. These fulfill the just requirements of the Sinai Law - plus, plus! The *"law of the Spirit of life in Christ Jesus"* can never lead us contrary to the Word of God. Jesus came "not to destroy the law but to fulfill it. He brings us from outer observance to inner obedience.

A Prayer

Lord Jesus, thank You for coming to us. Thank you for the New Life You have placed deep within our hearts. We want to follow you and be led by the Holy Spirit. Thank you for setting us free to go with You. We decide now to follow you and not to put adherence to tradition above our obedience to You. Amen.

CHAPTER 7

TRUE LIBERTY

We have seen that we are not saved *by* works but *for* works. When we receive the Lord as Savior and surrender our lives to His lordship, most of us are eager to move into the works He has for us. However, in our desire to be involved in His work and service, it is easy to get ourselves into projects and works that He has not appointed us to. It is also easy for us to slip into the attitude that our activities for God establish our relationship with Him. Our relationship with God is not attained nor maintained by religious activity, but by faith as a gift. At first this statement may seem almost shocking. To some, indeed, it will be shocking just as the story Jesus told about the Pharisee who put his trust in his religious activity and the publican whose only hope was the mercy of God, was shocking to the people of His day. (Lk 18:10)

In the letter to the Galatians, Paul wrote to a group of Christians who enjoyed great blessing when they first believed the gospel. They had experienced many miracles and demonstrations of the Holy Spirit's presence among them. It was glorious. Then something happened. The power of the Spirit waned and the beautiful sense of blessing and God's presence left. What went wrong? This group had enjoyed such joy and holy liberty in the presence of God and then it all seemed to dry up. (Galatians 3)

The message of the free gift of redemption through Jesus had brought them such joy and freedom. Now that joy was leaving them and their freedom was beginning to go. Apparently, some other Jewish believers in Jesus had come to them and told them that it was not enough for them to have faith in Jesus and His work on the cross. To stay filled with the Holy Spirit and to live pure and holy lives they must also keep the Old Covenant Laws.

> *Our faith is not in how good we are but in how forgiven and redeemed we are.*

The Galatian church continued in the freedom of the gospel until some false teachers told them that the only way to maintain their relationship with God was through religious activity. The freedom of faith began to be replaced by the strain of religious activity. They began to try to get closer to God by returning to the law of Moses and obeying all kinds of do's and don'ts. The effect of this was to bring them from a life of faith and trust in Jesus and the grace of God to a life of trusting in themselves. They were still believers. They still called Jesus "Lord" and professed faith in Him, but by their actions they were trusting more in themselves and their religious acts than in their faith in Him to maintain their life in the Spirit. Our faith is not in how good we are but in how forgiven and redeemed we are.

Paul expresses great concern that this corruption of the gospel was stealing their joy. He writes: *"You are severed from Christ, you who would be justified by the law; you have fallen away from grace."* (Gal. 5:4)

If we are reconciled to God and blessed through the saving work of Christ, going back to do's and don'ts (as holy as it seems) will sever rather than establish a relationship with God. The Galatians' fall from grace through a return to "do-it-yourselfism" has been repeated again and again throughout the history of the church. How often God has poured out His Spirit on humble and hungry hearts, only to have those people revert to all kinds of contrived religious activity to maintain their blessing and making laws out of their graces.

Some of the religious activity in the church today is a form of "going back under the law." It is an effort to establish or enhance a relationship with God through what we do for God rather than on what He has already done for us. If you have become a foolish Galatian, return to your first love and put all your trust in the grace of God and not in your conduct or knowledge. Let the presence of Christ manifest and shine forth radiantly in all you do. Often believers need to repent from religion (that is its self-righteousness and reliance on self-improvement through religious activity) as much as we need to repent of our sinfulness and sins. Remember that it was not through any obvious sins that the Galatians lost their sense of blessing but through going back to religious observance to establish or maintain their relationship with God.

Jesus foresaw that many believers would slip into this form of spiritual decay, which looks so godly when He warned: *"Beware of the leaven of the Pharisees, which is hypocrisy. Nothing is covered up that will not be revealed or hidden that will not be known."* (Lk 12:1-2)

Hypocrisy is often confused with insincerity. In fact, it is something quite different. Many hypocritical people are really sincere in what they are doing. Hypocrisy is the attempt to act differently than what one really is. In the process of doing this, one becomes deceived into thinking that he is the person he has been pretending to be. This is hypocrisy. It is a common disease among those who seek to be godly. It happens when people behave in a religious manner and thereby think that they have come close to God. The Galatians got infected with this disease, and Paul, therefore, warned them that godly behavior is the fruit of the Holy Spirit's presence in their lives and cannot be produced by religious striving, activity or pretense.

There once was a very happy married couple. They were deeply in love with each other, delighted to do many things for each other, and could never get enough of each other's company. The husband would work long hours to provide well for his bride and plan many special outings where they could be together. The wife, for her part, delighted in her homemaking and the thousand details that made their house into a home. Time went by and they still loved each other just as much.

Then one day they were invited to attend a marriage seminar. They did not really feel they needed the seminar but they went along anyway to please their friends. The counselor seemed very learned and knowledgeable about his subject. He spoke about communication, assertiveness, role conflict and all manner of subjects that our happy couple had never heard about. "If you do all that I tell you," said the counselor, who himself had had three marriages, "your marriage will improve greatly. Each day write down on a piece of paper all the faults you see in your spouse and at the end of each week show him the list. This will ensure open communication in your marriage." The happy couple took the counselor's advice. They noticed faults in each other and in themselves that they had overlooked before. They openly shared this with each other and then they began to defend themselves against these new accusations. The couple did not believe in divorce, but they separated and the communication between them collapsed.

A few months went by. They remembered the happy times that they had had together before they went to the marriage seminar. "Let's be simple," they said. "Let's just love one another and that love will teach us once again how to be one." They cried, they hugged, they laughed and from that day on, they lived in perfect harmony together.

The Galatians, like many of us, had the experience of falling in love with God through the message of the gospel and the work of the Holy Spirit, but had fallen back to legal works to create a relationship they already had and, in the process, weakened that relationship.

Today believers are returning to their first love. There is much teaching of do's and don'ts and complex psychology and theology that would steal us from the joy of our simple relationship with Christ. Teachers will come by with new formulas for holiness to try to make us work our way closer to God. We cannot get closer to God by any other way than the way that has been opened up by the cross of Jesus. Let us live in that happy position and from that position, let us bless and go to the people of our world.

What then is the place of religious activity in the life of the believer? When do we fall into the pitfall of the "foolish Galatians" and when are we exercising right Christian discipline? Whenever we use anything other than our faith in the work of Jesus on the cross to establish our relationship with God, we stray from a pure relationship with Him.

On the other hand, there is a right use of activity and discipline in the life of every believer. If, we use Bible study, church attendance and witnessing to express and celebrate the relationship with God that we already have, then these activities will uplift, encourage and strengthen the presence of Christ in our lives..

> We continue to 'abide in the Lord's grace by keeping His commandments, not by religious rules.

We continue to "abide" in the Lord's grace by keeping His commandments. *"If you love me,"* He says,

"Keep my commandments." (John 14:15) Again He says: *If you continue in my word then you are truly my followers and you will know the truth and the truth will make you free."* (John 8:31) His commandments show us how to live in relationship with God and with our fellow man so that we can live out and express the new creation life. It takes discipline and effort to continue to live a life of faith prayer, forgiveness generosity obedience and love, and every believer should be committed to live by these disciplines.

"Let us hold fast the confession of our hope without wavering, for He who promised is faithful; and let us consider how to stir up one another to love and good works, not neglecting to meet together as in the habit of some, but encouraging one another and all the more as you see the Day drawing near." (Hebrews 10:23-25). Just as a coal loses its heat when separated from the other embers of the fire so do believers who stay isolated from the rest of the Body of Christ becomes cold and their fire fizzles out. As believers we need to come together and to work together that we may grow in the knowledge and understanding of our relationship with God. We need to continually renew our minds and learn to walk in a manner that is according to our relationship with God.

Though we do not let any person or group usurp the primary place of Jesus in our lives we must learn to live in teamwork with other believers to fulfill our primary mission. As we live with others in the church, we learn to submit to the procedures and leadership of the groups with which we are associated. This is for right order because those in leadership have a responsibility to God and are placed in authority in the church by God to help us grow in grace and closeness to God. In these days, the true liberty of the Christian is threatened on the one hand by an undisciplined and self-indulgent life, and on the other extreme by a rigid legalism occasionally demanded by some in leadership who overstep the boundaries of their authority.

Be free, be humble, be a loving team player, be dead to the works of the flesh and you will always maintain a life of holy excitement experiencing daily the presence, power and the comfort of the Holy Spirit.

CHAPTER 8

THE LOVE PIPELINE

W hat is the most important thing in life? What is the greatest thing we can do on earth?

Once Jesus was asked a similar question. "Which is the greatest commandment?" He answered, *""You shall love the Lord, your God with all your heart and all your soul and with all your mind." This is the first and the greatest commandment. And the second is like it: "You shall love you neighbor as yourself." On these two commandments hang all the law and the Prophets."* (Matt. 22:37-40) He reduced the whole of man's responsibility to God and to man to these two commandments.

Religion tends to complicate things but real faith always simplifies. Today, as religious people divide and subdivide themselves along the lines of the minutest doctrinal distinctions, the words of Jesus were never more relevant. He reduces true faith and true religion to its most essential elements. The measure of godliness is not measured by denominational affiliation, your style of worship the way you dress, the size of your ministry etc., but by your love for God and your love of neighbor.

The goal of every human being is laid out in these two verses from Deuteronomy and Leviticus quoted here by Jesus: *"To love God with all our hearts mind and strength and our neighbor as ourselves."* Every other aspect of faith and religion is merely trimming. Every other spiritual exercise individually or collectively is simply a means of expressing or entering into this great reality. We have been placed here on this planet to love God and our neighbors as ourselves. We exist to love God and love others.

Notice that there are three loves referred to in these two verses.
- Love for God
- Love for ones self
- Love for others.

Each of these loves is "agape" love i.e. the God kind of love the love that is part of the nature of God and not part of the nature of man. It is as impossible for human beings to produce agape love as it is for pigs to fly. It is simply not a part of our nature. And yet God requires it of us. God asks us to do what we cannot do! This seems unfair. It would be if God Himself did not offer to help us to do what we cannot do naturally. He has "fixed us up" to be incapable of doing what He wants us to do apart from His direct supply.

The Love commandment cannot be fulfilled without God's help, God's life and God's supply. It cannot be lived without faith. *"For without faith it is impossible to please God" as without faith we cannot draw from the resources of God."* (Heb 11:2)

And so the law and the prophets that gave us the love commandment also revealed our incapacity to live by these commandments. They reveal the barrier of sin, which exists between us and God's love and supply. *"The law came through Moses and the prophet's grace and truth came through Jesus Christ."* (John 1:17) Since these commandments command us to love with a love we are incapable of, they bring us to the awareness of the bankruptcy of our own resources and the threshold of faith.

How can we who fail to live to God's standard access His resources? The answer is through the atoning sacrifice of Jesus who, as we have seen, took on Himself all our guilt, blame, sin and shame that we could have accesses to the Father's love. *"Justified by faith we have peace with God through our Lord Jesus Christ though whom also we have access by faith into this grace in which we stand and ... the love of God has been poured into our hearts by the Holy Spirit who was given to us."* (Romans 5: 1, 2 & 5)

This passage gives us insight into the mechanics of how the love of God works. Not only are we acquitted of our sins, but we also have access to the grace and resources of God our Father. Some believers stop short with the acquittal of sin, but God wants us to access His love. He wants us to access His love and resources just as the prodigal son coming home from His self-induced misery received not only pardon but also access to the resources of His father and access to His love.

Since the fall of man, we have become estranged from God's resources and life. This means that we are incapable of loving Him, our selves and others like we ought. Now through the cross of Jesus, we can access that love and be equipped to love God, love ourselves and love others. We access this love of God through faith and will. We can ask Him to pour His love into our heart through the Holy Spirit. We ask God to pour into our hearts

- agape love from God for God
- agape love from God for ourselves and
- agape love from God for others.

The Love Pipeline.

Faith in the atoning sacrifice of Jesus sets up a wonderful pipeline of love between us and God. God begins, through the Holy Spirit, to pour love from Him for Him, love from Him for ourselves and love from Him for others into our hearts.

This becomes a spiritual "pipeline" between God and us with three parts to it

- God's love coming from Him to us
- God's love circulating around our own innermost being
- God's love coming out of us to others.

In the pipeline we see three cut-off valves or taps that we control. If any of the taps are cut off, it reduces the flow of God's love to us in us and from us.

God's Love Through Us

If we have bitterness or unforgiveness towards others it stops the flow of God's love from us towards others. This simultaneously blocks the flow of love throughout the whole pipeline. This is why Jesus said if we have anything against anyone our relationship with God is blocked. *"And whenever you stand praying, if you have anything against any one, forgive him that your Father in heaven may also forgive you your trespasses. But if you do not forgive, neither will your Father in heaven forgive you your trespasses."* (Mark 11:25,26)

Paul reinforces this thought when He writes: *"Pursue peace with all men, and holiness without which no one will see the Lord, looking diligently lest anyone come short of the grace of God; lest any root of bitterness springing up cause trouble and by this many become defiled."* (Heb. 12:14-15)

It is up to us to keep the three parts of the pipeline open. We may have many people we disagree with, but we must ensure that while we disagree with them we harbor no unforgiveness or bitterness towards them so that our "pipeline" remains open. When we disagree with people, we must also forgive them, release them into God's care and ask Him to bless them and change them in whatever area He wants to change them. Secondly, we keep this part of the pipeline open by devoting ourselves to actively living for, helping and encouraging others as God directs us, in accordance with our individual gifts and callings.

Love For Ourselves

If we have self-hatred, self-rejection, inferiority, we also cut off the flow of God's love *within* us and this causes the flow of His love to us and though us to be blocked. All of us have picked up some patterns of self-rejection before the love of God was poured so wonderfully into our hearts through the Holy Spirit. We have to recognize the negative images or words (planted in our hearts and heads through "the father of lies") we have entertained in the past about ourselves. We then replace them with the Lord's total acceptance and love (His agape) poured into our hearts *for ourselves* - the unique person He made created and formed to lavish His love on. We now must continue to "abide in" God's love, allowing His love to circulate within us and put away all patterns of self-hatred and self-rejection.

Acceptance by God brings us peace with Him, peace with ourselves, and peace with others. When we don't have this peace with ourselves and love for ourselves we are prone to depression, insecurity, anxiety, envy, depression, anger etc. In our confusion, we can compound our problems by seeking love and affirmation in the wrong way or in the wrong places. We can succumb to work-aholism, materialism, sexual disorder, driven-ness etc.

God's Love To Us

As we have seen the atoning sacrifice opens a way for all to come and receive the love of God though faith. This flow of love, from God to us, must be

> *This flow of love from, God to us, must be maintained by constantly believing and drawing from it.*

maintained by constantly, believing and drawing from it. The greatest difference between human beings and animals is not in our intelligence or speech. The difference is that only we have a capacity for a relationship with God. We were made for relationship with God and with each other. The atoning sacrifice restores us into a personal loving relationship with God and God's love is communicated to us directly through the Holy Spirit. *"And because you are sons, god has sent forth the spirit of His Son into your hearts crying out "Abba Father.""* (Galatians 4:6) This love satisfies man's deepest needs. Being in relationship with God we can now trust Him with our present our past and our future. We can live without fear and anxiety and in great hope.

Spiritual Warfare

The devil, or accuser, tries to suggest to us directly by thoughts injected into our consciousness or through the words or behavior of others towards us that God does not really love us or care for us. He came to Jesus to make Him doubt that He was in special relationship with God the Father *"If you are the Son of God"* he said to Jesus. Immediately Jesus silenced Him saying: *"Get behind me Satan!"*.

We, too, can silence the devil's voice when he tries to make us doubt God's love for us. In the past, we may have agreed with the thoughts and suggestions of "the father of lies" (John 8:44). We can now cancel any agreement we have made with him when we agreed with his assessment of us. We can resist him now and stand boldly in the full sunshine of the Father's love for us. (We know we do not deserve this love, which He freely gives us, but we gladly and boldly accept it.)

A Prayer

Father, thank you that through the Blood of Jesus my sins are atoned for. I now come to You to stand in Your grace and in your love. Through the Holy Spirit pour into my heart
Your love for me
- love from You, for You
- love from You, for myself, and
- love, from You, for all men.

Help and empower me to love You, love myself, and love others in a complete and full way all the days of my life.

CHAPTER 9

THE TREE OF LIFE

To solve a problem it is always best to look for the remedy at the problem's point of origin. The Bible tells us that man's problems (i.e. yours and mine) came about when we ate of the "Tree of the Knowledge of Good and Evil." (Genesis 3:7) How could eating of the fruit of a tree be the source of so much trouble? Eating of the Tree of the Knowledge of Good and Evil marked a departure for the human race. When man ate of this tree we chose to control our lives by our own thoughts, opinions and ideas rather than by living in dependence upon and obedience to God.

We have chosen to live

- by our own understanding and
- in independence of God rather than
- living by His directives (His Word and
- in dependence on Him.

"All we like sheep have gone astray; we have turned everyone to his own way BUT the Lord has laid on Him the iniquity of us all." (Isaiah 53)

Adam and Eve sinned by going their own way and caused us to inherit the curse of separation from God's intimate presence. Jesus became obedient to death and restored all who come to Him to intimacy with God. *"In Him we have redemption through His blood, the forgiveness of sins according to the riches of His grace."* (Ephesians 1:7)

When we are restored into God's presence through faith in the Blood of Jesus, we must learn to live a life of faith and trust, by being guided by God's Word and Spirit. If we are to stay close to the Lord, we must stay away from the "Tree of The Knowledge of Good and Evil" and remain dependent on God and obedient to His directives. This is the new obedience to which every believer is called. As the proverb says: *"Trust in the Lord with all your heart and lean not on your own understanding. In all your ways acknowledge Him and He shall direct your paths."* (Proverbs 3:5) *"Behold the proud, His soul is not upright in him, but the righteous shall live by his faith."* (Habakkuk 2:4)

The only way we can please God is if we cease from leaning on our own opinions and live by faith – in childlike trust and obedience to God.

"Assuredly I say to you unless you repent and become as little children you shall by no means enter the kingdom of heaven" says Jesus (Matt. 18:3) If we are to please God there is no more important message than the life of faith.

The life of faith can only be understood if we know the lesson of the two trees in the Garden of Eden: The Tree of Life and The Tree of the Knowledge of Good & Evil.

The Obedience Of Faith

When we put our faith in the work of Jesus on the cross and receive His forgiveness, we can also lay down our old selfish "Adam" life and receive Christ's resurrection life in exchange. When this new life of Christ comes into us, we learn to walk in a new pattern of obedience to Him who is now our Head and Leader. The old obedience was obedience to external regulations; the new obedience is to the directions of the Head, Jesus. Paul called this new obedience, *"the obedience of faith."* (Romans 1:5).

Many see God's redemptive work entirely in terms of His powerful acts of mercy and rescue of us though the Cross. Yet God has a fuller purpose in His plan for each of us. His purpose is that we would live in obedience to Him just as Jesus lived, and that in so doing we would show forth His character and life.

Paul, who had a mighty ministry in proclaiming the redemptive work of Jesus, described his ministry as bringing people to *"the obedience of faith"* (Romans 1:5) God saves us to bring us under His rulership because we can only

> It is vitally important to each of us that we learn to be led by the Holy Spirit and the Word of God in all that we do.

enter into His fullness if we are in subjection to Him. This obedience of faith comes about as we learn to submit to the teachings of the scriptures and to follow the inner direction of our new spiritual hearts. In the walk of faith, there is never any question of following external voices. The Spirit of God will always speak in line with the scriptures. It is vitally important to each of us that we learn to be led by the Holy Spirit and the Word of God in all that we do. The Spirit and the Word work together like the two aim lines of a rifle. When the Spirit and the word line up we will hit God's target

"For all who are led by the Spirit of God are sons Of God" (Romans 8:14). There is no more important lesson for the believer than to learn how to be led by the Spirit for this is the life we have been called to in Christ.

The First Bite Of The Tree of Knowledge

In the Book of Genesis, the scriptures tell us

how man's fall from fellowship with God came about. Adam and Eve had been placed in a beautiful garden to live. Their every need was supplied there, and they were able to consult with God about anything they needed to know. (Genesis 3:8) However, they did not have the kind of union that we can now enjoy in the kingdom of God. In the kingdom of God, in the realm of the new creation, we know God through His Spirit who dwells *within us.* In the first creation, Adam and Eve spoke to God *outside* of themselves. In the new creation, we have been lifted up into such union with God that as long as we abide in that union, God dwells in us and we hear His voice.

Everything was beautiful and peaceful for Adam and Eve in their garden paradise. *"And the Lord God planted a garden in Eden in the east; and there He put the man whom He had formed. And out of the ground the Lord God made to grow every tree that is pleasant to the sight and good for food, the tree of life also in the midst of the garden and the tree of the knowledge of good and evil. And the Lord God commanded the man, saying: "You may freely eat of every tree of the garden; but of the tree of the knowledge of good and evil you shall not eat, for in the day that you eat of it you shall die.""* (Genesis 2:8-10,16-17.)

Some time after this, the tempter, in the

form of a serpent, said to the woman, *"You will not die. For God knows that when you eat of it your eyes will be opened, and you will be "**LIKE GOD**, knowing good and evil"* (Genesis 3:4-5). Adam and Eve were in fact already "like God" since they were made in His image and likeness. (Genesis 1:26) They maintained the image and likeness of God as they lived in **communion** and **dependence** on Him. Satan tempted them to feel incomplete and to look for something apart from God, when they were already complete in Him. He contradicted the Word of God saying that they would not die if they ate of the Tree of The knowledge of Good & Evil. *"For God knows that in the day you eat of it your eyes will be opened and you will be like God knowing good and evil."*(Gen. 3:50) They wanted to know good and evil for themselves apart from dependence on and consultation with the Lord.

We are all familiar with the outcome. Their eyes were opened, and they fell from their happy position of fellowship with God. Taking a closer look at what happened, we can see that their fall was caused by a desire to be *like* God knowing good and evil. It was not eating of any ordinary fruit tree that brought about their fall. The decision they made was to have their lives guided by their own knowledge and understanding of good and evil rather than the voice of God and this brought about their downfall.

This has been the primary sin of man ever since Eden. We prefer to be guided by our own clouded minds rather than by the clear voice of God. Man has never had a desire to do evil as such. We can assume that Adam and Eve had no direct motive towards evil. Even in their desire to know good and evil for themselves apart from the guidance of God, their intention was surely to choose good and avoid evil. Since that time man has, for the most part, guided his life by his own understanding of what is good or evil rather that the voice of God.

The Place Of The Mind

The mind is, obviously, one of the greatest gifts that God has given us. Most people would see nothing wrong in the attempt to guide one's life by understanding and reason. To this day this is the prevailing way by which men guide their lives. This kind of humanism is dominant in today's western culture. As wonderful as the gift of intellect is, man was destined from the beginning to be guided by God through His Spirit and Word.

Man is a spirit who has a mind, and who lives in a body. Man's spirit was made for fellowship and communication with God, and through this communication was to guide his life.

When we share this truth, people are

surprised. They think that when we say we should be guided by something higher than our minds, we are being anti-intellectual. This, of course, is not true. The mind has a huge part to play in our lives, but it is not *the highest* authority. If we were to assert that though our eyes are a

> As wonderful as the gift of intellect is, man was destined from the beginning to be guided by God through His Spirit and His Word.

great and wonderful gift, they are not to be the source of our decisions and choices, no one would accuse us of being against the use of our eyes. When the scriptures teach that we should be guided by something (Someone) higher than his own mind, they are not, against the right use of the mind. They are simply against any attempt by the mind to take the place of God.

The Spirit of Heaviness

Sometime ago, we became aware of the lack of joy, and the emotional and mental heaviness we observe in some believers. As we pondered these things, the Holy Spirit brought to our attention the events of the fall of Adam and Eve from the Garden of Eden. We saw that New Creation men and women often make the same mistake as first creation man and woman. We, too, eat frequently from "The Tree of the

Knowledge of Good and Evil" rather than abiding at "The Tree of Life" to which we now have access.

When we eat of "The Tree of the Knowledge of Good and Evil", we are guiding our lives and judging our situations by our reasoning minds instead of by the Spirit and Word of God. Whenever we put our minds above God's Word and voice, we are eating of the Tree of Knowledge of Good and Evil. When Adam and Eve did this, they lost their fellowship with God and their position in the garden of Eden.

Sometimes when we consider the sin of Adam and Eve, we may think that it is really unfair that we should be the victims of their sin. We may think that should we ever be in a similar situation we would never do what they did. The fact of the matter, however, is that we *do* continually make the same mistakes *they* made whenever we choose to be led by the knowledge of good and evil (our own opinions and choices) rather than by the Spirit and the Word of God.

The scriptures say: *"Trust in the Lord with all your heart, and lean not on your own understanding. In all your ways acknowledge Him, and He shall direct your paths."* (Pv. 3:5-6) However, the mind of the natural man rebels against submitting to the higher wisdom of God as revealed in His word. *"The natural man does not receive the things of the Spirit of God, for they are foolishness to him, nor can he know them because they are spiritually discerned."* (1 Cor. 2:14)

The "Good" Is Not "The Best"

Often we believe that if we can succeed in "doing good and avoiding evil" we will automatically be pleasing God. The world is full of "good" people and "nice" people who are dedicated to doing good and avoiding evil but who are yet not in the kingdom of God nor led by the Spirit of God.

The kingdom of God is not only the realm where we live under the *care* of God, it is also the realm where we live under His *authority*. While we are busy doing "good" things and "important" things we can miss the "best" thing. If we are living at the level of "The Tree of the Knowledge of Good and Evil", we shall be satisfied with doing "good" things. However, in so doing we can completely miss God and become "workers of iniquity". *Many will say to Me in that day, "Lord, Lord, have we not prophesied in Your name and cast out demons in Your name, and done many wonders in Your*

> *While we are busy doing 'good' things and 'important' things we can miss the 'best' thing.*

136

name?" And then I will declare to them "I never knew you, depart from Me, you workers of iniquity."" (Matthew 7:22-23)

The apparently "good" religious things that these workers have done are unacceptable to God because they have their origin in their own good ideas and are not from the heart of God. They were done simply from their own initiative and not in submission to the Lord. Religious goodness can be as far away from the plan of God as evil. God is bringing us back under the Lordship of His Son so that our actions may be rightly aligned with His plan. It is often more difficult for "good" people to come under the Lordship of Jesus than evil people because openly "evil" people more readily acknowledge their need.

Our call is not a call to "do good and avoid evil", but a call *"to hear the Word of God and keep it,"* (Luke 11:28) and to be led by the Spirit of God. *"For all who are led by the Spirit of God are sons of God."* (Romans 8:14). The "good" man does "good" things; the religious man does religious things, but the man of God does God's things.

Of all the thousand and one *"good"* things we could be doing, how can we select the ones we are really called to do? The only way we can make the right choices is through being led and guided by the Spirit of God into those works and activities that God Himself has appointed to us. *"For we are His workmanship, created in Christ Jesus for good works, which God prepared beforehand, that we should walk in them."* (Ephesians 2:10) In the kingdom of God, we let God do the choosing. He will never choose anything evil for us to do, of course, but there are many good things that He will not assign us to.

The Sentryman

Can you imagine a soldier joining an army and then engaging himself in every aspect of the work there? If the soldier were to involve himself in another man's assignment, he could cause much confusion for himself and others. The sentryman, for example, must remain at his post when all is calm and quiet even if the cook could use more help in the kitchen.

To be involved in good activity is not enough. We must also know that we are doing that which we have been assigned by God. No member of the body acts independently of the Head. If any member acted independently, the result would by chaotic.

> Good activity is not enough. We must do that which we have been assigned by God.

Imagine what would happen if our eyes were to decide to take a rest when we are driving home at night, or our legs decided to take a walk when we are trying to talk to a friend. Yet we see much of this erratic and uncoordinated behavior in the Body of Christ because the various parts of the body choose to make their own decisions so often rather than being guided by the Head.

No Passive Minds

God wants us to be led directly by Him, rather than by the choices of our independent thinking. He has a higher purpose for our actions than that which the mind can conceive. The surrendered believer uses his mind to choose those directives revealed by the Spirit and the Word, and to test each one with the scriptures to be sure that he is really hearing the Word of God.

In all of this, the mind, though it freely subordinates itself to the Word of God and the Lordship of Christ, does not remain passive or blank. The mind investigates what is written in the scriptures and distinguishes between the voice of God and that of the clamoring pressures of the world. The believer

> *The Christian uses his mind and will to choose to obey and yield to God's choices and directives.*

also renews his mind through the engrafted Word and tests all things with the scriptures and the Holy Spirit.

Finally, the believer uses his mind and will to choose to obey and yield to God's choices and directives. The mind has indeed a most important part to play in every Christian's life. We do not suppress the mind, but subordinate it to the leadership of Christ.

Believers function through a subordinated mind. This is a mind that is freely and deliberately subordinate to the Lordship of Christ as revealed through the Spirit in harmony with the scriptures. This does NOT mean that the Christian should blank out his mind and receive every thought and suggestion that comes into his mind as if it were the voice of God.

Some believers fall into a passive state of mind and do not keep it active in its right place. They act as if they did not have a mind and are, therefore, open to deception. In this state they may fall into the trap of surrendering their decision- making to some other person, or even to demon spirits, as happens in some cults.

Though we are to be led by the Spirit and not by our minds, we are to *engage* our minds in our search for the mind of God in any particular matter.

We do this by
- searching the scriptures
- listening to the witness of the Spirit in our hearts
- praying for clearer guidance from the Lord

- listening to the advice of pastors and mature friends in the Lord
- releasing our own likes and preferences
- renewing our consecration, and by
- choosing God's choice.

To be led by the Spirit is not something "spooky" or super mystical. For the man in Christ, it is *naturally supernatural and supernaturally natural* because God has written His laws "deep within our hearts" at the time of our new birth. Since His Spirit has come to abide in us, the voice of God is nearer to us than we are to ourselves.

The Peace In Our Hearts

When we were born from above, our spirits became one spirit with the Spirit of Christ, for *"he who is* united *to the* Lord becomes one *spirit with Him* "* (I Cor 6:17.) Just as our body "speaks" to us when it needs rest or food, so too our spirits, when united to the Spirit of the Lord, speak to us when the Lord wants to direct us in anything. When we are in the will of God, or when the Lord wants us to continue on with what we are doing, He gives us deep peace in our hearts. *"Let the peace of Christ rule in your hearts to which indeed you were called in the one body"."* (Colossians 3:15).

God communicates to all who are born again. Jesus said, *"My sheep hear my voice, and*

I know them and they follow Me." (John 10:27) This speaking is not generally in an audible voice or prophecies but in the gentle nudging of His Spirit within us. God can, of course and sometimes does, speak in an audible voice or through a prophecy, but even these forms of communication will serve only to confirm the inner nudging of the Spirit within our hearts and will never be a substitute for it.

> *Those who are led by the Spirit of Jesus will also be led by the words of Jesus.*

Those who are led by the Spirit of Jesus will also be led by the words of Jesus. Jesus said: *"He who hears these words of mine and does them is like a wise man who builds his house upon a rock."* (Mt. 7: 26) The believer builds his life on obedience to the words of Jesus and the direction of the Holy Spirit. Since the Holy Spirit is the author of the Scriptures and so His directives will always be in harmony and in line with the scriptures. The true inner witness will always agree with the witness of the scriptures

The Salmon & The Perch

Once there was a handsome young salmon that had been spawned in a mountain stream in Ireland. How he enjoyed his mountain streams and the deep pools and splashing waterfalls. As time went by, however, he began to feel somewhat uneasy. The stirrings of adventure began to move deep within him and the desire to travel the vast salt ocean began to awaken within him. Swimming downstream with the rapid current of the river he began his long, long journey - a journey that would take him across the vast waters of the Atlantic even to the far off exotic islands of the Caribbean.

More time went by, and the desire to return home now began to stir within him. He began to swim north by northeast. He did not really know exactly which direction he was moving in, he just knew he was headed towards the tinkling streams of his Irish hills. And so he returned.

When he returned, the stories of his travels were circulated among the fish that swam and lived in the mountain lakes and streams. Among them was an ambitious young perch. He heard of the exploits of the salmon and he decided to emulate them. He prepared for his journey meticulously, by much study of oceanography and navigation. Finally, he too set out on his journey of adventure. Filled with confidence, and sure of his calculations and preparations, he began to swim as no perch had ever swam. Soon he was unmistakably lost and hopelessly confused. The perch knew more about navigation than any salmon and yet he was lost. He had been guided by his learned knowledge while the inner law of his being had guided the salmon.

The "John The Baptist" Experience

John the Baptist was beheaded for the sake of the gospel. Many of us need to be "beheaded" in a spiritual sense. We must learn to subordinate our "heads" to the will and word of God.

When we are born again, the inner life of God's Spirit is implanted deep within us. As we obey this new inner law, "the law of the Spirit of life in Christ Jesus", we will fulfill God's plan for our lives. However, the programming of our intellect or the pull of our emotion tend to pull us away from this law. So we must continue to remain attuned to this new inner law, which is far more intelligent than our highest reason or the lust of our emotions, and test everything with the written Word of God.

The Happy Life

As we live at the Tree Of Life we return to this law of God and submit our emotions, opinions and wills to the will and word of God. This is the key to a life of unspeakable joy and blessing.

Jesus says that if we "seek first the kingdom (i.e. the counsel) of God and His

> *Trust and obedience are the believer's secret of a happy life.*

righteousness and all these things will be added to you." (Mt. 6:33) This is an echo of God's words through Moses. *"If you diligently obey the voice of the Lord your God to observe carefully all His commandments, which I command you today.. all these blessings shall come upon you."* (Deut. 28:1-2) Trust and obedience are the believer's secret of a happy life. To be led by the Spirit we put our minds in second place and surrender our beings to the highest guidance principle of all - God Himself, who made us to be guided and directed by Himself and not by our own intellect.

By restoring us to open fellowship with Himself and placing His law within our hearts, God has brought us back to The Tree of Life. He has redeemed us from The Tree Of The Knowledge Of Good And Evil - the source of our confusion and striving.

What Is Sin? - *It's Not What You Think It Is*

The revelation of The Tree Of Life gives us insight into the origin and consequence of sin. From this we can see how this truth applies to our lives today.

Sin has traditionally been presented as violation of the moral code especially as described in the Ten Commandments. And so the moral person is regarded as *not being* a sinner and the immoral person is regarded as *being* a sinner. Redemption is presented as the forgiveness of violations of the moral law; and the new birth is presented as the inner empowerment (through the dwelling of Christ) to live the moral life.

There is much truth in this traditional explanation but it is not the truth. It is highly inaccurate and has resulted in Christians having a very diluted understanding of what our redemption is.

The traditional view creates several problems.

1.   The morally good person does not see any need of redemption.

2.   The Christian who is living a morally good life does not lay hold of the fullness of redemption.

3.   Redemption is seen only as God's answer to the *moral* problem and not his answer to the *sin* problem.

If sin is only moral lapse then the purpose of redemption is to provide forgiveness from the penalty of our moral lapses and empower us to have no more lapses. Sin is not primarily a matter of moral lapses. It is the *condition* man is in when he has become separated from the life glory and presence of God. Anything we do that removes us from God's presence is sin, and anything we do when removed from God's presence and life bears the mark of sin.

Paul writes *"anything that is not of faith is sin."* Anything that does not look to the resources of God for its accomplishment misses God's standards. Sin is neither immorality nor evil. It includes immorality and evil but it is more than that. It came into the world before immorality and evil came into the world. Adam's sin was *not* that he chose evil. (Genesis 2 & 3) He ate of The Tree Of The Knowledge Of Good Or Evil

a) to become as God

b) to know good and evil for himself apart from God

c) to become independent from God.

As we have seen, the devil who tempted him tried to make him doubt what he already had. He was already *as* God because he was made in the image and likeness of God. As he remained in receptive dependence on God he bore God's image and likeness. All man's knowledge and power came directly from God. In separating himself from God's Presence he felt naked, realizing that he had moved away from God's glory.

> *All the consequence of sin – separation from God's presence, God's wisdom, God's glory, Gods' life, God's wisdom and God's resources – are a result of man's decision to live independently. from God.*

All the consequence of sin – separation from God's presence, God's wisdom, God's glory, Gods' life, God's wisdom and God's resources - are a result of man's decision to live independently from God.

It is not that Adam stopped believing in God. He still believed in God's existence in His identity as Creator etc., but he deliberately chose to live His life in INDEPENDENCE from God. In separating himself from God's presence life and resources.

- death came in
- moral decay came in
- sickness came in, and
- work became hard and heavy.

Sin & The Ten Commandments

Moral decay is only *one* of the *symptoms* of sin. The Ten Commandments were given to *restrain* immorality and to *give knowledge* of sin but, as we have seen, they had no power to restore the closeness that man once knew with God.

Jesus' redemption brings covering and cleansing for the defilement of sin. *"Though your sins be as scarlet they shall become as white as snow though they are red like crimson, they shall become like wool."* (Isaiah 1:18) His redemption restores us back to the relationship of closeness that Adam had with God. The new creation relationship is even closer than Adam's relationship because now God comes to dwell in the heart of believers. Here there is forgiveness for moral lapses, and an impartation of a sinless life. The redemption brings us back into union with God and His resources. It brings us out from the misery of separation into the blessing of being in His full care.

Righteousness, Sin & Self- Reliance

Sin is self-reliance - relying on our wisdom, (natural or theological) our strength and our power.

Righteousness is not only moral correctness but leaning on God's power life and wisdom, so that His power life and wisdom are displayed through us. This can only come through Jesus, the Way, the Truth and the life. The gospel is more than the message of sins forgiven. The mystery of the gospel is Christ **_in_** us as the hope of glory. He lives in us as the source and reality of our righteousness, our relationship with God and our wisdom.

"Christ is given to us as wisdom sanctification and righteousness." (1 Cor. 1:30) As the lampshade has no light of its own but displays the light of the bulb within so to we have no righteousness of our own but can reflect the righteousness and life of Christ within us.

Sin & Self

Sin is the operation of self in separation from God. All progress in the Christian life involves increased knowledge of self. Specifically the knowledge that self without God will always fail to please God and meet God's standards. Progress consists in realizing the bankruptcy of self that we may learn to expect nothing from self and expect everything from God. God takes no delight in our humiliation and failure, but He uses them to make us turn away from self and onto Him. New Testament Repentance is more than turning from sins; it is the act of turning away from self to Christ.

The religious man can be as far from God as the immoral man. His self-righteousness is just as sinful as the immorality of the immoral man. (It is just as sinful to live at the "good" side of the "Tree of Knowledge" as it is to live at the "evil" side of it). This is why Jesus' message was more easily understood by immoral folk who were aware if their sin than the self-righteous who were not so aware. *"Blessed are the poor in spirit for theirs is the kingdom of heaven."* (Matt. 5:3)

> *The religious man can be as far from God as the immoral man.*

Much of Christendom knows Jesus only as the sin bearer. Having their sins forgiven they then try to do better in the power of self.

Deliverance from sin is not simply deliverance *from immorality* but deliverance *from self and its strength; self and its goals, and self and its wisdom.* What makes something sin or not is not whether it is good or bad, but whether it has its *source in self or with God.*

Everything that has God as its source pleases Him, and everything that does not cannot.

- Man in self (in Adam) is corrupt in all he does.
- Man in union with God participates and displays the divine character.

It is important that we know how debased we are when we are in self and how glorious we are when in total dependence on God.

Redeemed From Good And Evil

Let us now take another look at these two spiritual trees that are mentioned in the book of Genesis, the Tree of Life and the Tree of the Knowledge of Good and Evil. We have

"*Since believers are so self-reliant, self-boasting and self-satisfied God would rather see them sin that do good. Otherwise they shall never know themselves, nor shall they ever be delivered from the pitiable sometimes laughable, yet abhorrent self-life.*" Watchman Nee.[1]

already seen that God has made us to be guided and directed by His Spirit and Word, and not by our reasoning minds i.e. our own understanding of good & evil (The Tree Of The Knowledge Of Good And Evil.)

The Paralysis of Analysis

Not only are our lives not to be directed by our minds alone, but they are not to be *analyzed,* measured, or judged in terms of "good and evil" either.

Many live their lives with regrets about the past. They blame themselves for mistakes they have made or perhaps they feel that their lives have been ruined or thwarted by various injustices or "bad breaks". We *can*, of course, analyze all the events that have gone into our lives in terms of good and evil. We can analyze our position and condition today in terms of good and evil. To do so, however, is not helpful.

If we analyze our past history in terms of good and evil, we might perhaps assess it as follows: "I had a reasonably good childhood but my parents neglected certain matters in their care of me, as a result of which... or "My childhood was partly good and partly bad. I am happy about the good parts, but I regret the bad parts, for there is nothing I can do now to undo the damage. My education was also partly good and partly bad. I am happy that I had some wonderful teachers, but others were not so good and did much damage to my self-confidence, etc. etc."

Many tend to analyze their life experiences in these terms. They see their lives as a mixture of good and bad, of ups and downs. Each day is seen as partly good and partly evil, and so it is reckoned as partly successful and happy and partly the opposite. Since this is the way they consider life to be, they resign themselves to being partly happy and partly unhappy, partly frustrated. Even the happiest of men have had some evil touch their lives, or make some irreversible mistakes at some point, and so even they consider themselves to be partly victims of the evil that is in the world.

> *Analysis of our lives in terms of good and evil may be quite accurate and true, but it is not helpful and produces hopelessness and regret.*

This kind of analysis of our lives in terms of good and evil may be quite accurate and true, but it is not helpful and produces hopelessness and regret. We can come away from this Tree Of The Knowledge Of Good And Evil. We can leave the realm of analysis, regrets and "if only's" and come to the Tree of Life, which is the realm of faith. Here the Lord's redemptive touch changes everything that has gone into our life and causes it to work for our good. *"And we know that all things work together for good for those who love God, to those who are called according to His purposes."* (Romans 8:28)

Four Explanations Of Our Problems

If we choose to live in the realm of the Tree of the Knowledge of Good and Evil, there are four possible explanations we can give to explain every difficult circumstance in our lives.

1. We can blame them on ourselves
2. We can blame them on someone else (parents, teachers, social systems, political leaders, church leaders, spouse, employers, enemies, etc.)
3. We can blame them on the devil
4. We can attribute them to God

Usually, if we attempt this kind of analysis of our problems, we will come up with an explanation that is a combination of some or all of these. Such explanations may be accurate, but they have little power to remedy the situation.

The One Way Street Of Blessing

If we come to the Tree of Life on the other hand, we come to the realm where we release ourselves into the realm of God's mighty working and redeeming ability and away from our vain analyses and futile regrets. Instead of apportioning blame and "licking our wounds", we yield all situations into the hands of God who makes "all *things work together for good for those who love* Him" (Romans 8:28). This is the amazing condition and privilege of those who live in the kingdom of God. Here in this realm ALL things, yes, ALL things, the evil as well as the good are working together for our good as we abide in Him and continue to release all to Him.

> Lordship of Jesus everything in our lives becomes a blessing.

Instead of living on the two-way street of good and evil, believers can now live in a wonderful dimension where we are on a one-way street of blessing in which everything is a blessing to us. We can truthfully say: *"From now on, and for the rest of our lives we shall never meet a person or a situation that is not going to be a blessing to us"*. Everything that will happen to us and every person we shall ever meet is going to be a blessing to us as long as we remain under the Lordship of Christ our Redeemer, and continue to surrender all things to God for Him to bless, use and redeem.

We are certainly not saying that we can never be touched by evil again or that we have discovered some magic vaccine that immunizes us from evil. What we are saying is that *we can never encounter a situation, which God won't turn into a blessing for us, if we abide at the tree of life.* Jesus never promised that life with Him would be immune from evil. *"Sufficient for the day is the evil thereof,"* He said. (Matthew 6:34) He also said that we would have tribulation in this world, but that tribulation would not destroy us and would work for our good (John 16:33).

Our lives may be touched by the evil that is still in the world, but as we remain in union with Him, that evil will not destroy our lives but will actually be made to work for our good. *"I have said this to you that in me you may have peace. In the world you have tribulation; but be of good cheer, I have overcome the world"* (John 16:33).

> It is not what happens to us so much as how we react to what happens to us that makes it a blessing.

Whenever we turn our evil situations over to God for Him to use, He works in it for our good. It is not what happens to us so much as how we react to what happens to us that makes it a blessing. This is not a mere positive thinking technique, but the true response of one who is living in faith in God's ability to turn all good and evil things into blessings for us.

> God can make it better that the bad thing happened than if it had never happened.

In the church we talk much about Jesus as

our Savior and about Jesus as our Lord. We need also to allow Him to be continually our Redeemer. He is the one who can take all that has gone into our lives, and all that is now going on in our lives, **under His control** and use it all to advance His purpose in our lives, and to bless us if we let Him.

He takes all of the evil that has touched our lives, whether it was caused by ourselves or by others, and, *as we release it to Him,* makes it better that all these things happened than if they never happened. – **What a Redeemer!**

Beyond Psychology

In today's society there is much emphasis placed on discoveries made in the realm of psychology and psychiatry. To understand things from a psychological point of view can be of help to some. It is often a help and a crutch for the natural (Adamian) man. However, for the New Creation believer, psychology can become a temptation to "munch" from The Tree Of The Knowledge Of Good And Evil.

Most psychologists regard the harmful effects of lacks, deprivations and wounding experiences in our lives as minuses to us. They may help us to recognize, admit and confront these "lacks" and teach us how to live with them. However, the more we analyze in this realm, the more evident our "minuses" become. While the psychologist may help us to cope with the hurts of our lives, no modern psychological technique can heal the wounds to our psyche like the redemptive work of Jesus as we abide at The Tree Of Life.

When we come away from the realm of analysis, introspection and blame apportionment that is the mark of those who live at The Tree Of The Knowledge Of Good And Evil and come to Jesus, all our "minuses" (psychological and otherwise) can be turned into pluses. As we

- release all to His touch
- receive His forgiveness and
- in turn, forgive others,

we are released from the hurts of the past and their effects on our lives. It is then that we can truly experience that God does make all things work *together for good for those who love Him* - even deprived childhoods and hurtful experiences - as we release all to the redemptive touch of Christ.

Jesus – Our King Midas

Most of us are familiar with the legend of King Midas. He was granted the fulfillment of his wish that everything he touched would turn to gold. Whatever he touched turned to gold. If he were to touch a bushel of silver, it would turn to a bushel of gold; if he were to touch a bushel of trash, it too, would turn to gold. No matter what came in contact with his fingers, valuable or worthless, it would turn to gold.

The legend of King Midas is, of course, only a story, a piece of fiction. The story of King Jesus, our Redeemer king, is far from being a mere story. It is the central fact of history. As we give Him the scars of our lives, He turns them into the gold of blessing. Give Him our happiness, and He will make it a twice-blessed happiness. Give Him our pains and sorrows, and disappointments, and He will turn them into assets, *"For my strength is made perfect in weakness"* (2 Corinthians 12:9). As our Redeemer, He not only redeems us from our sins, but He touches all the evil, and injustices and mistakes of our lives and makes them work for our good.

No More "If Only's"

It is critically important that we come away from The Tree Of The Knowledge Of Good And Evil. If we remain at this tree, our lives will remain filled with bitterness and regret. Surely the fruit of this tree is more bitter than the most bitter herb. As we eat from it, it fills us with regrets and "if only's." ("If only I had studied harder at school," "If only my parents had had more income," "If only I had made a different career choice," "If only I had not been treated so unfairly," "If only I had invested my money differently," "If only...") At the Tree of Life, we come away from all our "if only's" to Jesus with His redemptive touch, and we see Him take all that has ever gone into our lives, forgive us of our personal liability, and make it all work for good.

Let us not look at the cross of Jesus, and imply by our regrets that He did not do enough. *"It is finished"* (John 19:30). He is more than a conqueror over all the good and evil in our lives. *"Who shall separate us from the love of Christ? Shall tribulation, or distress, or persecution, or famine, or nakedness, or peril, or sword? As it is written, "For thy sake we are being killed all the day long; we are regarded as sheep to be slaughtered. No, in all these things we are more than conquerors through Him who loved us. For I am sure that neither death, nor life, nor angels, nor principalities, nor things present, nor things to come, nor powers, nor height, nor depth, nor anything else in all creation, will be able to separate us from the love of God in Christ Jesus our Lord."* (Romans 8:3,5-39).

The Power To Forgive

It is only in the dimension of the Tree of Life that we can truly forgive and live the forgiving life. Often we try to forgive but our minds remain filled with regret that this unwanted event took place. We say, *"I forgive"*, but inside we are thinking: *"I want to forgive, but that person has done me much harm, which can never be undone."* However, when we KNOW that God takes the injustices, the heartbreaks and the disappointments of life into His mighty hands to make it better that they happened than if they had never happened, then we KNOW that the painful experience can become a blessing in our lives. In this context it is easy to forgive as we release all to Him.

The Example Of Joseph

A great example of this truth is found in the Old Testament in the life of Joseph. (Genesis 37-50) When Joseph received the coat of many colors from his father, his brothers became violently jealous. They threw him in a pit and sold him to some wandering merchants who took him off to Egypt. All kinds of injustices befell him there. He was wrongfully accused and thrown into jail. Yet God used all these apparent misfortunes, promoted Joseph to a very high place of influence and finally used him to rescue his entire family.

Joseph must have wondered why all these things were happening to him as he went through these testing experiences. Perhaps he thought that there was some deep flaw in his personality or that he had done something to remove himself from the blessing of God. Perhaps the devil had destroyed the promise of his early years or that he was the victim of a bad family or bad court and prison system.

If Joseph ate of the Tree of the Knowledge of Good and Evil, there is no doubt that his mind would have wandered down all these negative labyrinths. However, Joseph did not rebel against all these inexplicable misfortunes that seemed to continually befall him. He did not eat of The Tree Of The Knowledge Of Good And Evil but entrusted his cause to God. In the end he was able to say to his brothers, *"Fear not, for am I in the place of God- As for you, you meant evil against me; but God meant it for good, to bring it about that many people should be kept alive as they are today."* (Genesis 50:19-20). Joseph knew that what man and the devil and the circumstance of life had been directing towards evil, God had been directing to work for good in his life, for his own sake, the sake of his family, and the nation of Israel. This is the privilege of all who trust God steadfastly.

The Example Of Jesus

The greatest example of this truth, however, is Jesus Himself especially in the events of His crucifixion and resurrection. Before He finally submitted to this dreadful fate, Jesus went to His Father to inquire once more if there was any way in which He could avoid it. *"Father, if thou art willing, remove this cup from me; nevertheless not my will but Thine be done"* (Luke 22:42). Later before Pilate, He said: *"You would have no power over me unless it had been given you from above."* (John 19: 11) By this, He showed that He was receiving it from His Father above and not from secondary causes.

From the point of view of the knowledge of good and evil, we would say that the death of Jesus was evil. We would say that Jesus was the victim of the disloyalty of His followers, the betrayal of Judas, and the corrupt state of the religious and political establishment. If ever the devil had caused anything, this surely was his work.

Jesus, however, did not live in the realm of the Tree of the Knowledge of Good and Evil, but received all things through His Father's hands releasing everything to Him. We know that God took all these evil events and turned them around to work our redemption. What the devil intended as evil, God used for the good of all of us. Even from the standpoint of Jesus' personal life, God used those who were the instruments of His death to press Him on to resurrection and our redemption. *"Jesus for the joy that was before Him endured the cross, despising the shame, and is seated at the right hand of the throne of God."* (Hebrews 12:2).

Abide in Him, and see yourself no longer in

the up and down life of those who live in the realm of The Tree Of The Knowledge Of Good And Evil. As a believer, you are now in the kingdom of God. See yourself as being under the care of God and under the Lordship and redemptive ability of Jesus Christ where all things are working together for your good.

As we come away from the double vision of The Tree Of The Knowledge Of Good And Evil, we can come into the blessed single vision that Jesus spoke about. *"The eye is the lamp of the body. So if your eye is single, your body is full of light" (*Matthew 6:22). God wants us to see all things in the light of His Lordship and Redemption, and to be able to say with the apostle Paul: *"Who shall separate us from the love of Christ? Shall tribulation, or distress, or persecution, or famine, or nakedness, or peril, or sword? As it is written, For thy sake we are being killed all the day long; we are regarded as sheep to be slaughtered. No in all these things we are more than conquerors through Him who loved us. For I am sure that neither death, not life, nor angels, not principalities, nor things present, nor things to come, nor powers, nor height, nor depth, nor anything else in all creation, will be able to separate us from the love of God in Christ Jesus our Lord" (Rm. 8:35-39).*

A Prayer

Lord, we release to you all that has gone into our lives, the good and the evil, the disappointments and the triumphs, every injustice that anyone has done against us, any mistaken decision we may have taken.

We receive your forgiveness and forgive ourselves and all who may have harmed us and trust You to redeem all the liabilities of our lives completely, and make them work together for our good. Amen.

CHAPTER 10

CONQUERING THE LIAR

When Jesus was anointed with the Holy Spirit, the Spirit led Him into the wilderness of Judea for a period of fasting. These days were days of preparation and decision for Him. During this time He encountered the devil and was tempted in various ways. As we read the account of this period in His life we can see how totally committed He was to be led by God's Spirit in everything He did - even when that leading contradicted His own desires. The temptations, which Jesus encountered are, however, not unique to Him. Every spirit-filled believer must face the same temptations and overcome them if he wishes to be led by Spirit into a life that is effective for God.

One might expect that once a person is "born again" and "baptized with the Holy Spirit" that his battles are over. The opposite is true. The infilling of the Holy Spirit not only clothes us with power, it also equips us for spiritual conflict.

Let us look at Jesus' temptations and see them not just as something that was part of His own personal history, but as a pattern for the kind of temptations that all sincere disciples of His face. *"And Jesus, full of the Holy Spirit, returned from the Jordan and was led by the Spirit for forty days in the wilderness, tempted by the devil. And He ate nothing in those days; and when they were ended, He was hungry. The devil said to Him, "If you are the Son of God, command this stone to become bread."*

"And Jesus answered him, "It is written, Man shall not live by bread alone." And the devil took Him up, and showed Him all the kingdoms of the world in a moment of time, and said to Him, "To you I will give all this authority and their glory; for it has been delivered to me, and I give it to whom I will. If you, then, will worship me, it shall all be yours."

"And Jesus answered him, "It is written, You shall worship the Lord your God, and Him only shall you serve." And he took Him to Jerusalem, and set Him on the pinnacle of the temple, and said to Him, "If you are the Son of God, throw yourself down from here; for it is written, He will give His angels charge of you to

guard you, and On their hands they will bear you up, lest you strike your foot against a stone.""

"And Jesus answered him, "It is said You shall not tempt the Lord your God." And when the devil had ended every temptation, he departed from him until an opportune time. And Jesus returned in the power of the Spirit into Galilee." (Luke 4:1-14).

Here we read of three major temptations the devil tempted Jesus with and tempts us with also. The first temptation, to turn stones into bread, can be seen as an attempt to get Jesus to concentrate on the pursuit of material prosperity before obedience to the promptings of His heavenly Father and the Word of God.

The second temptation, in which Jesus is offered all the kingdoms of the earth was an attempt to draw Him into the pursuit of social and political power before obedience.

The third temptation, in which Jesus is asked to jump from the pinnacle of the temple to show His faith, can be seen as an attempt to draw Jesus into reckless acts that God His Father had not called Him to. This too would have been another form of disobedience. Here He was being tempted to presume on God's miracles without obeying God's

> *The things with which the devil tempted Jesus were things, which His Father would give to Him in due, time.*

169

principles.

The most subtle thing about these temptations is that each of the things with which the devil tempted Jesus were things which His Father **would give to Him anyway in due time.** It was definitely God's will for Jesus to have all the bread He needed. It was also God's will for Jesus to be over all the kingdoms of the earth. These are already His legal dominion and will soon be seen to be His.

His temptation was, and ours is, to pursue the things which God wants to give us in due season rather than pursue the will of God. Jesus was not to pursue these things; He was to inherit them. He said: *"The meek shall inherit the earth",* (Matthew 5:5) and He asks us to learn meekness from Him. He has set us a pattern and an example of meekness and obedience. *"Take my yoke upon you and learn from Me, for I am gentle and lowly in heart and you will find rest for your souls"* (Matthew 11:29).

In His temptation period, Jesus decided not to pursue anything on His own but to obey His Father. He knew

Jesus decided to pursue obedience to His Father and not the things His Father would give Him, as the first goal of His life.

that as He did this, His Father would bring Him

into His inheritance. He knew that He could ask and receive anything He needed from His Father without compromising His commitment to put God's will, God's plan and God's purposes first. Jesus deliberately decided to pursue obedience to His Father and not the things His Father would give Him, as the first goal of His life. Our temptation too is to pursue that which the Father wants to give us, rather than obedience to Him.

Jesus summed up the lessons of His temptation when He said: *"The Gentiles seek all these things; and your heavenly Father knows that you need them all. But seek first His kingdom and His righteousness, and all these things shall be yours as well."* (Matt. 6:32-33).

Many today have no idea they are falling for the temptations of the devil when in fact they are. They have Jesus as their Savior. They have received reconciliation with God through the Cross and they have been filled and baptized with the Holy Spirit. They would not dream of making any sort of deal with the devil and would never deny the Lord. Yet they unwittingly yield to the devil's temptations.

How can this be? How can the devil influence the behavior of born again, Spirit baptized Christians? He uses the same methods he tried unsuccessfully on Jesus. He spoke to Jesus through His lustful, self-serving desires, but Jesus did not respond to these desires. The devil speaks to us in the same way through our lustful, self-serving desires. If we are not watchful we may think: "I am a believer in God. The blood of Jesus redeems me. All things are lawful for me and I have scripture to back up my desire to go this way."

The unsuspecting believer can pursue the course of action suggested by his own lustful desires and unwittingly fall into the devil's trap and veer off the course of obedience to the heavenly Father. James tells us that when we are tempted by the devil, he tempts us through our lustful desires. *"Let no one say when he is tempted, "I am tempted by God"; for God cannot be tempted with evil and He Himself tempts no one; but each person is tempted when he is lured and enticed by his own desire."* (James 1:13-14). We can see that when Satan tempts us, he does so through our carnal desires.

When Peter urged Jesus to avoid the Cross-, Jesus recognized it as the same temptation He had faced in the desert. This time it was being voiced through the sentimental concern of His friend, Peter. Jesus answered: *"Get behind me Satan! For you are not on the side of God but of men"* (Mark 8:33).

From James' letter we learn that temptation works through our selfish carnal desires. From the exchange between Jesus and Peter we see that temptation is present whenever we look out for our own interest even when it conflicts with God's plans and strategies for us. And so we can observe that to serve self's interests, when those interests do not coincide with God's, is to fall for the devil's temptations.

Times of temptation are permitted in our lives so that we may face what is within us and deliberately choose to put God's interests and ways above our own. Even if those choices may sometimes result in short-term loss and humiliation, we know that in the end it will be the happiest and best way for us. If anyone chooses to take this path of integrity and faithfulness, God guarantees that in due time all of those good things that he is willing to postpone for the sake of obedience to Him, will be added.

> *Times of temptation are permitted in our lives so that we may face what is within us and deliberately choose to put God's interests and ways above our own.*

Obedience to God involves tough choices at times for all followers of Jesus. These choices may cause some short-term losses, but in due season they will result in enduring rewards. *"If any man would come after me, let him deny himself and take up his cross and follow me. For whoever would save his life will lose it; and whoever loses his life for my sake and the gospel's will save it. For what does it profit a man to gain the whole world and forfeit his life?"* Jesus (Mark 8:34-37). Later He says: *"Truly, I say to you, there is no one who has left house or brothers or sisters or mother or father or children or lands for my sake and for the gospel, who will not receive a hundred fold now in this time, houses and brothers and sisters and mothers and children and lands, with persecutions, and in the age to come eternal life. But many that are first will be last and the last first."* (Mark 10:29-31).

God does not object to our having power and land in this life. However, if there is a conflict between these things and the demands of God and His gospel, obedience to God must come first. He assures us that whenever radical obedience to God's call and standards cause loss, in time, HE will more than compensate for the loss. In fact, He will repay a hundred fold.

There is a journey to be made between the promises of God and their fulfillment that can only be made through the pathway of obedience. The devil tempts us to pursue the promises without taking the pathway of obedience and to miss God in the process. Each of us must make the choices that Jesus made in the wilderness if we are to follow Him. He allowed the devil to expose every tendency to evil that was in Himself. Then He faced up to those weaknesses and decided not to be ruled by them.

These decisions He took at the beginning of His public ministry made Him sensitive to any recurrence of these temptations amid the busyness of His public ministry. Because He had faced these temptations head-on in the lonely silence of the desert, He was able to recognize them later as they would recur and not be seduced by them.

Obedience was to be His pathway to His glorious position and success and not the pursuit of success itself or the trappings of success. *"Let each of you look not only to his own interests, but also to the interests of others. Have this mind among yourselves, which you have in Christ Jesus, who, though He was in the form of God, did not count equality with God a thing to be grasped, but emptied Himself, taking the form of a servant, being born in the likeness of men. And being found in human form, He humbled Him self and became obedient unto death, even death on a cross. Therefore God has highly exalted Him and bestowed on Him the name which is above every name, that at the name of Jesus every knee should bow, in heaven, and on earth and under the earth, and every tongue confess that Jesus Christ is Lord, to the glory of God the Father."* (Phil. 2:4-11).

At first, it seemed that the path of obedience was a path of total loss, but in the long run, it resulted in ultimate, permanent victory and exaltation for Jesus. The choices, which Jesus made in moments of temptation, are to be made by all of us, especially those who have been anointed with His Spirit. Jesus has already won the battle over the devil and self for all of us, but it is to be lived out and worked out in our lives through simple obedience.

Overcoming Harmful Thoughts

The account of Jesus' victory over the devil in the wilderness illustrates how He dealt with harmful thoughts and ideas.

His victory also shows *us* how *we* can overcome the dark thoughts and evil spirits which all of us have to deal with from time to time. *"He who overcomes **as I also have overcome** I will grant to sit with me on My throne."* (Rev. 3:21) If we want to rule with Him we too must learn to overcome as He did.

Jesus defeated the devil at the Cross. We do not have to defeat him again, but we do need to *resist* him. The devil is the father of lies and he works through lies. He, and the lower spirits that

> *Though the devil is defeated, he still must be resisted.*

serve him, try to recover authority over us by lying to us. Our task is to refuse the lie and replace it with the truth. *"Submit yourselves therefore to God. Resist the devil, and he will flee from you."* (James 4:7)

When He was in the wilderness, Jesus was bombarded with delusional thoughts. However, He was not deceived because He quickly recognized these thoughts (and the emotions they generated) were neither truthful nor in line with God's word. He recognized these thoughts did not come from within Himself, but were being transmitted towards Him by an evil spirit – Satan. He therefore refused to come into agreement with the lies and commanded the spirit behind these lying thoughts to leave Him.

The Believer's Authority.

"Behold, I give to you authority to tread on serpents and scorpions, and over all the authority of the enemy. And nothing shall by any means hurt you." (Luke 10:19)

Jesus gave His followers the authority to resist the evil spirits that work on the earth to harass, intimidate, discourage, deceive and accuse us in the same way that He did. *We have* complete authority through Jesus over these spirits and to walk in this authority and use it whenever necessary

"These signs will follow those who believe in My Name, they will expel demons."(Mk 16:17)

The first sign to accompany a believer, according to Jesus, is the ability to expel demons.

This may seem strange to our modern mind, but in fact it is very practical. Like it or not we live in a world where there are many evil spirits operating in the unseen realm. Because we live in a spiritual world we have to deal not only with unhealthy thoughts but also with the spirits that transmit these thoughts. Jesus' experience in the wilderness clearly shows this.

That is why John writes *"Beloved, do not believe every spirit, but test the spirits to see whether they are from God, for many false prophets have gone out into the world."* (1 John 4:1) Believers can be bombarded with tormenting thoughts such as thoughts of despair and discouragement, which can lead to depression and even suicide. Similarly they can be assailed with unclean thoughts, which can lead to destructive sexual behavior, or with thoughts that incite envy, bitterness and vengeance. These thoughts can come to us directly to our spirits or through the countless information bytes that compete for our attention each day

However, because Jesus has given us authority we need not be afraid. Instead of being passively dominated by these thoughts we now have authority. We are equipped through the authority and Name of Jesus to resist all negative thinking and lying thoughts. We refuse, just like Jesus did, to come into agreement with thoughts that are not in line with God's word and ways and we commands the spirits behind these thoughts to leave us in Jesus' Name.

The strategy of the enemy is to cause us to agree with a lie. Deny the lie and he loses the basis of his effort to control or influence us.

> *Deny the lie and the enemy loses the basis of His control.*

Most of us have entertained and agreed with untrue and unhealthy thoughts for years. Such thoughts accessed us through our culture, family history and the hurtful experiences of life.

These thoughts become the devil's prison which entrap us in a world of despair and darkness. Once we are in Christ however the prison door is open. We are now in a new realm and we can deal with negative thoughts in a new way. We recognize them as lies, eject them from our consciousness and command any spirit associated with them to leave.

In Jesus' case the devil came back with similar thoughts at a later time. As the scripture says, *"He left Him until an opportune time." (Luke 4:13)* The same is true for us. Even when we resist negative and delusional thoughts and command the spirits behind them to leave, these thoughts may reoccur at some later stage. We simply continue fill our minds with the truth of God's Word and continue to resist the lie and the lying spirits.

"When the unclean spirit has gone out of a person, it passes through waterless places seeking rest, and finding none it says, "I will return to my house from which I came." And when it comes, it finds the house swept and put in order. Then it goes and brings seven other spirits more evil than itself, and they enter and dwell there. And the last state of that person is worse than the first." (Luke 11:24-26) This story shows how evil spirits can return. However, if we have filled our minds with the word of God and continue to resist, they will not be able to regain entrance to our lives.

The authority that Jesus gave us to use His Name against dark spirits, that come to oppose us, is one of our greatest privileges. Countless lives would be saved from destruction if all believers knew how to
- cancel agreement with ungodly thoughts (form the past or present) and
- command the spirits, which transmit these thoughts to leave us in Jesus Name.

A Prayer
Yes, Lord, I decide to follow you that Your plans for my life may be fulfilled. Enable me by Your Spirit to follow You faithfully. I know that as I seek obedience and faithfulness to

You, everything else in my life will fall into place.

I cancel agreement with all thoughts, attitudes and emotions that I have come into agreement with in the past that are contrary to your ways.

I command every spirit that has sought to oppress me with negative thoughts, unclean thoughts, thoughts of despair, delusion, bitterness, envy despair and hatred to leave me now in Jesus' Name. Amen.

Christianity Without Religion

CHAPTER 11

BLESSED AND A BLESSING

The predominant revelation of God in the Bible is that He is a God of love and mercy. God is unspeakably good and wonderful. He delights in doing well for all that call on Him - for all His children. *"I know the plans I have for you plans for you welfare and not for your harm to give you a hope and a future."* (Jeremiah 29:11) The tragedy is that we have chosen to go our own way rather than embrace God's wonderful will and plan and take shelter in His care. This has brought us under the partial dominion of the devil and has separated us from God's blessings so that sickness, poverty and sin hold sway over the earth.

God warned the Israeli people (under the Sinai covenant) that if they did not adhere to the moral and ritual laws of the Covenant, they would become vulnerable to physical, emotional and political disaster. At the same time, God was aware that because of the weakness of our sin infected human nature, no one could ever perfectly keep these laws. And so, as He gave the laws of Sinai, He also gave the system of Sacrifice by which sins would be forgiven and atoned for. *"And the priest shall make atonement for him before the LORD, and he shall be forgiven for any of the things which one may do and thereby become guilty."* (Leviticus 6:7)

The idea here was the principle of substitution - which is that symbolically; the guilt of the person would be transferred to the animal. These animals, we now know prefigured the death of Jesus - the Lamb of God - who was to come and take on Himself the guilt, sin and sickness of all of us.

The great theme of the New Testament is that God loves sinners like you and me so much that He interposed His beloved Son Jesus to take the blame, the shame, the guilt, the pain, and the emotional and physical curse, which are the consequences of our sin. (John 3:16)

"He was despised and rejected by men; a man of sorrows, and acquainted with grief; and as one from whom men hide their faces He was despised, and we esteemed Him not. Surely He has borne our griefs and carried our sorrows; yet we esteemed Him stricken, smitten by God, and afflicted. But He was wounded for our transgressions, He was bruised for our iniquities; upon Him was the chastisement that made us whole, and with His stripes we are

184

healed All we like sheep have gone astray; we have turned every one to his own way; and the LORD has laid on Him the iniquity of us all." (Isaiah 53:4-6)

Redeemed From The Curse of The Law

As Isaiah clearly foresaw, the Messiah (Jesus) took on Himself our sins pains griefs. Jesus not only took our sins but He took the cursed consequence of our sins upon Himself. *"Christ has redeemed us from the curse of the Law having become a curse for us that the blessings of Abraham may come upon us Gentiles through faith."* (Galatians 3:20) The Messiah, Jesus, redeemed us from the curse of the Law: poverty, sickness, and disease by taking that curse upon Himself.

He became sick that we could become well.

He was despised and rejected of men so that we could be accepted and find favor.

He was stripped of all His reputation and goods.

He became poor that we might become rich.

He took our poverty and disgrace that we could be adopted into the family of God, become joint heirs with Him and live in the realm where there is now no barrier between us and the provision and blessing of God. This is an essential part of the good news.

We can now live under the canopy of God's love, blessing and provision. We can stand in the full sunshine of His love as we have seen, and we can live in the blessing of His provision for our lives. God takes us out from the curse of separation and into the realm of His protection and blessing. *"My God will supply every need of yours according to His riches in glory in Christ Jesus."* (Phil. 4:19)

His blessing and keeping power extends also to our bodies. *"The Lord is for the body and the body for the Lord."* (I Cor 6:13) *"I am the Lord that heals you."* (Exodus 15:26) He is the God who heals and provides. Everyone who returns to the Lord through Jesus is no longer under the dominion of sin, sickness or poverty,

- Our sins are forgiven
- our diseases have been removed
- our bodies healed
- and we live in the realm of God's abundant provision.

John puts it this *way "Beloved I want you above all to prosper and be in health even as your soul prosper."* (3 John 1) God wants us to be in good health and to prosper as our soul prospers.

- Our souls prosper as we allow love kindness and joy replace selfishness, indifference and depression.
- Our souls prosper as we cut ourselves off from the agenda of our selfish ego and bind ourselves to the purpose and plans of God for our lives.
- Our souls prosper as we keep our thoughts filled with what is positive and what is good.
- Our souls prosper as we allow love to fill our hearts and minds and we cut off from our lives envy jealously bitterness and unforgiveness.

The whole world is invited, Jew and Gentile to put our faith in the great fact that Jesus has taken our curse and to come home to the blessings of God our loving Father.

Because it is God's will that our lives succeed in the purposes for which He made us and that we be kept free from sin and sickness can learn how to appropriate these blessings and realities by faith.

1) We know that God loves us so much that He sent Jesus to take our guilt sin and sickness.

2) We accept what God has done for us in Christ Jesus in simple and childlike faith.

3) We study the Word of God concerning this to establish in our own minds and hearts what truly is God's will in these areas.

4) We remove any practice in our attitude that hinder the blessing of God in our lives.

We enter into the realm of God's blessing through faith. This faith is not just agreement to the theological factors of redemption, but by putting all our trust in the Lord, by adhering to His ways. Faith lays hold of God's promises and waits for God to fulfill His word. Faith is not discouraged by delay or by temporary setback. Faith is not afraid of delay. *"Faith comes by hearing and hearing by the word of God."* (Romans 10:17) Faith comes when we allow the word of God to penetrate our hearts and minds and to reveal God's wonderful will to us.

The blessings of God (including health, purpose and provision) come upon us not as we pursue them as the main goal of our lives but as we pursue the will and purpose of God for our lives. They come when we place ourselves in trust under His care and commit ourselves to walk in His ways. *"Seek first the kingdom of God and His righteousness and all these things will be added to you."* (Matthew 6:33)

Receiving the blessing of God on our lives requires that we lay hold of the promises and ask God for the faith to receive *and take* what He is giving. It requires that we remove bitterness, unforgiveness, resentment and envy from our lives so that the love and blessings of God can flow through us. *"If you abide in me and words abide in you,"* Jesus says. *"You may ask anything and it will be done."* (John 15:7) If we do not abide in love His blessing cannot continue to flow in our lives.

The life of faith is not one of magic but of entering into God's blessing. The blessing of health also requires that we abide in God's love and God's ways, that we treat our bodies properly as temples of God's Spirit and that we exercise, work, rest and eat in moderation.

Trusting God for our health does not preclude the judicious use of medicine as our bodies and lives are coming into fuller alignment with God. The same is true when we trust God as our Great Provider for financial provision and blessing. Some people think that they can believe God for financial blessings without being willing to work and apply themselves. The scriptures require that we work and live lives of service. *"For even when we were with you, we gave you this command: If any one will not work, let him not eat."* (2 Thess 3:10) Those who do not work and serve cannot expect God to meet their needs. God also promises in a special way to be the provider of those who are most needy and of those who are generous. "You will be enriched in every way for great generosity (2 Cor. 9:11*) "The*

Generous soul will be made rich and he who waters will himself be watered." (Proverbs 11:25)

The Promises of God

Peter tells us God has given us *"precious and very great promises that through these we may escape the corruption that is in the world through lust." (1 Pt 2:6)* We should meditate on these promises and lay hold of them by faith asking God to supply faith to live by His ways and appropriate *His promises. "O taste and see that the Lord is good Happy is the man who takes refuge in Him !"* (Ps 34:8) How the Lord wants to take care of us. He yearns that we trust Him for every area of our lives. How He yearns that the world would know the riches of His goodness and learn to come to Him, lean on Him and look to Him to provide all our needs for spirit, soul, and body and to making our lives a blessing on the earth.

The Scriptures say that God's *people "perish for lack of knowledge"* (Hosea 4:6) Through ignorance of God's word and promises many believers fail to lay hold of God's call God's hope and God's promises and so they do not have an anchor for their faith and for their prayer.

"Bless the Lord O My soul and forget not all His benefits,

Who forgive all your iniquities

Who heals all your diseases

Who redeems your life from destruction

Who crowns you with loving-kindness and tender mercies

Who satisfies your mouth with good things so that your youth is renewed like the eagles. (Psalm 103:2-5)

How often believers forget or ignore these wonderful benefits which God wishes to pour out on us. When we do not remember these benefits we fail to ask God for them. He will not force His favors on us. We must receive the truth of His word as little children and trust Him to fulfill His promises in our lives. We ask and keep on asking that His will, as it is revealed in His Word, will manifest in our lives. God truly wants to be a loving caring Father for us in every area of our lives.

"You do not have, because you do not ask." (James 4:2) *"Hitherto you have asked nothing in my name; ask, and you will receive, that your joy may be full."* (John 16:24). God reveals His word to us so that we can ask and receive form Him what He wants to give and do for us.

The Keys of the Kingdom

The blessings of God and of His kingdom come our way as we pray and use the keys of the kingdom of heaven. Jesus said to His disciples (and therefore to us) *"I give you the keys of the kingdom of heaven and whatever you bind on earth will be bound in heaven and whatever you loose on earth will be loosed in heaven."* (Matthew 16:19 & 18:18)

God could overwhelm us with His power but chooses not to bypass our wills. He waits for us to ask Him to do what He wants to do. Prayer is not the means of imposing our will on God but of opening up our hearts to His good will, and to the blessing, purposes and directions He has for us.

When we take the keys of the kingdom - the prayer principles of binding and loosing -

- we can loose ourselves from everything in our lives that is outside God's will, and bind ourselves to all that is God's will.
- We can loose ourselves from the agenda of self and bind ourselves to the purposes and calling of God for our lives.
- We can loose ourselves from all hurts and emotional hang-ups that block the fruit of the spirit in our lives and bind ourselves to the reactions of Christ.
- We loose ourselves from any thoughts and attitudes that are not in line with the mind of Christ and we bind ourselves to the mind of Christ.
- We loose ourselves from all unforgiveness and bind ourselves to forgiveness.

As we do this we enter into God's will and purposes for our lives and align ourselves to the situations and attitudes He can bless.

The Tribulation Principle.

Though it is God's will to heal and provide for all His children, all believers go through tribulations. *"I have said this to you, that in me you may have peace. In the world, you **have tribulation**; but be of good cheer; I have overcome the world."* (John 16:33)

At such time, it may seem that God's blessing is withdrawn from our lives. Believers can go through long periods where the blessings of health and provision seem to be withheld or blocked. Often there is an identifiable blockage such as unforgiveness or bitterness that we can identify and deal with, but sometimes the reason is beyond our capacity to understand. Consequently, believers should never assume that because another believer is sick or has financial difficulties that it is always their own fault or that they have not enough faith.

Occasionally believers can pass through tribulation, like Job, only to emerge more blessed than ever before. It was also the case for Joseph who was especially blessed by God but also went through a long period where it did not SEEM that he was blessed. And so while believers should always proclaim that God is our great provider and healer, we should not condemn those who are going through tribulation. At the same time, we should not allow the tribulations or struggles of others to rob us of our faith in the promises of God.

Removing Blockages To Blessing

When God's blessings do not seem to come through, some people lose faith or try to interpret the Bible to fit their experience, by saying that it is not God's will to heal and to bless everyone.

Sometimes, as we have seen, the problem is beyond our knowledge, and we should not play Job's comforters to those who are in tribulation. One day every believer will be totally healed and blessed in every way. The task today is to get as much of God's will done on earth as we can. Knowing God has a higher benign will, we can continue to look to Him to perform His will and fulfill His promises in our lives. The benefits opened up by the Atoning work of Jesus can flow into our lives only through the channels of faith and prayer.

Jesus says *"whenever you stand praying, forgive, if you have anything against any one"* (Mark 11:25) Paul says, *"let a man examine himself"* (I Cor 11:28) and further writes that *"those who are in the flesh cannot please God."* (Romans 8:8) He lists such things as strife, envy, covetousness etc. as *"works of the flesh"* and says that *"those who practice such things will not inherit the kingdom of God"* i.e. receive the benefits of the kingdom. (Galatians 5:19-21) The works of the flesh, according to Paul, are major blockages to blessing in the lives of believers.

As we ask God's will to be done in our lives we must recognize, take responsibility for, and remove any blockages in our lives to blessing. Some major blockages to blessing are: unforgiveness, bitterness, broken-heartedness, guilt, resentment, violation of God's moral laws, occult involvement, anti-Semitism, self-hatred, fear, generational curses (i.e. inherited misfortunes coming upon us because of the sins of our ancestors) and unbelief.

Healing The Broken-Hearted

Healing broken hearts is a major part of Jesus Ministry. *"The Spirit of the Lord is upon me,"* He said, *"because he has anointed me to preach the gospel to the poor; he has sent me to **heal the brokenhearted**, to preach deliverance to the captives, and recovering of sight to the blind, to set at liberty them that are bruised."* (Luke 4:18) All whose hearts have been broken by life's events can call on Jesus Himself to heal their broken hearts. He can fill the void left in hearts by bereavement, abandonment, rejection disappointment and grief.

All of us have had some of the these blockages in our lives. When we

- recognize
- take responsibility
- repent,
- renounce
- remove these things from our lives, and
- receive forgiveness and cleansing from these things through the Blood of Jesus we can remove the blockages.

It is essential, for example to forgive everyone who has ever hurt us, (including ourselves) and release them into God's care.

As we remove these blockages we loose ourselves from the negative effects of these sins, bondages and blockages and place ourselves in the realm where God can bless. We can then invite God, Our Loving Father, to pour His love through the Holy Spirit, into all the wounded corners and cavities of our hearts.

It is important, also, to formally loose us from the sins of our ancestors (including idolatry, false religion, occult involvement and membership of organizations such as Freemasons). We can declare our liberty through Jesus' Blood and Atonement from any misfortune their oaths, sins and mistakes may have made us vulnerable to,

Faith keeps hoping and believing and never gives up. Hebrews Chapter 11 records how many through faith did great exploits, while others did not receive the fulfillment of their faith but, yet, they still persevered in faith. Abraham *"not being weak in faith he did not consider his own body already dead (since he was about a hundred years old) did not waver at the promise of God through unbelief but was strengthened in faith giving glory to God and being fully convinced that what He had promised He was able to perform."* (Romans 4:19-21) Faith in God's Word enables us to look beyond circumstances to the God of miracles. We can look beyond the seen to the unseen and trust God to fulfill His promise.

God yearns to bless His people and make us a blessing. God said to Abraham that He would bless him and make him a blessing (Genesis 12:4.) Paul says *"Christ has redeemed us from the curse of the law having become a curse for us that the blessings of Abraham might come upon the Gentiles in Christ Jesus."* (Galatians 3:13-14) Believers in the atoning work of Jesus are not only released from the curse of the law - they are blessed and become a blessing to others. What a destiny!

A Prayer For Blessing

Lord thank You for redeeming me from the curse of the law through the atoning death of Jesus on the Cross. Thank You Jesus for not only taking my sin upon Yourself but for also taking my pains, sickness and all that separated me from the blessings and provision of God. I let all my griefs sorrow and pains go to You,. I know that as blotting paper absorbs ink so You can absorb my sickness and sorrows which I now let go to You. I place myself and my family under Your Headship to live my life in the realm of Your blessing and care in the Father's house. I take You as my Redeemer, Healer and Provider and I release my spirit, soul, and body into Your care. I am forgiven. I am Healed I am blessed thanks to You.

I renounce and remove myself from the works of the flesh and I declare that I am free through the Blood of Jesus from all curses or misfortunes coming upon me through oaths or any false religion, occult activity or sins of my ancestors back to third and fourth generations and I declare my Liberty in Jesus name

CHAPTER 12

HOPE FOR THE WORLD

The year 1967 marks a pivotal year in world history. In that year the City of Jerusalem came back under Jewish dominion for the first time since 70 AD The regathering of the Jewish people to Israel the Land of promise was foretold by the prophets and by Jesus Himself. Jesus foretold that Jerusalem would lay desolate under Gentile control for many years and that He would return shortly after the return of Jerusalem to Jewish control. (Matt. 24 & Luke 21)

The times we are living in, are therefore the *"time of the harvest"* and *"the end of the age"*. They are the most exciting times in history. It is a time that the prophets, apostles and early disciples longed to see. It is the time of the denouement of the age and the climax of history. These times *are* special, and have been uniquely referenced in the scriptures.

The disciples asked Jesus what would be *"the sign of His coming and the end of the age"* (Mt. 24:3) and He responded to them by giving them a prophetic dissertation concerning the future of Jerusalem and the Jewish people. He prophesied four major events

1) That Gentile armies would destroy the city

2) That the Temple would be destroyed

3) That the Jewish people would be scattered all over the world and

4) that they would be regathered to Jerusalem and that Jerusalem would come back under Jewish control. (Luke 21:24)

The answer Jesus gave to the question of what will *"the sign of His coming be and of the end of the age"* was specific, historical and verifiable. The end of the age would not be until these four verifiable events took place.

Jesus also said: *"They will fall by the edge of the sword, and be led captive among all nations; and Jerusalem will be trodden down by the Gentiles, **until** the times of the Gentiles are fulfilled.* (Luke 21:24)

The key word here is "until". Jesus predicted that Jerusalem would be under gentile domination - but not forever. Eventually Jerusalem would be returned to Jewish rule. This was the sign by which we would know we were at the end of the age.

The end of the age should not be confused with the end of the world. It is the end of the present age, which began with Jesus" Ascension and will end with His return as King of Jerusalem and King of the world.

In the year 70 the Roman army took possession of the City of Jerusalem destroyed the city and the temple and sent the Jewish people into exile. From then until 1967 Jerusalem languished under Gentile control. No one except the students of the Bible ever believed that the Jewish people would come home to their possession in Jerusalem. But Jesus had foretold that it would happen before His return. According to Jesus' own words (quoted above) His triumphant return could not happen until Jerusalem came back under Jewish control. Isaiah prophesied

We now know from the words of Jesus that since 1967 (the year Jerusalem came back under Jewish control) we are in the end of the age. Jesus also said that the end of the age is the time of the harvest *"The harvest is the end of the age."* (Matthew 13:39)

Isaiah Jeremiah Ezekiel and other prophets had also declared that the Jewish people would return a second time to their land.

*"In that day the Lord will extend His hand yet **a second time** to recover the remnant which is left of His people, from Assyria, from Egypt,*

from Pathros, from Ethiopia, from Elam, from Shinar, from Hamath, and from the coastlands of the sea. He will raise an ensign for the nations, and will assemble the outcasts of Israel, and gather the dispersed of Judah from the four corners of the earth. (Isaiah 1:12-14)

*"Then I will gather the remnant of my flock out of all the countries where I have driven them, and I will **bring them back** to their fold, and they shall be fruitful and multiply."* (Jeremiah 23:3)

*"I will set my eyes upon them for good, and I will **bring them back** to this land. I will build them up, and not tear them down; I will plant them, and not uproot them."* (Jeremiah 24:6)

These events of the restoration of Israel and Jerusalem foretold more than two thousand years ago are taking place before our eyes in an incredible way. From the ruins of the Holocaust came the restoration of Israel. God is preparing the events of History for the age of the kingdom. Since this generation has witnessed the restoration of Jerusalem to Jewish authority,

> *Since this generation has witnessed the restoration of Jerusalem to Jewish authority, we can categorically say that now is a time like no other time - it is the end of the age.*

202

we can categorically say that now is a time like no other time - it is the end of the age.

Jesus said that the end of the age would not only be a harvest of good but a harvest of evil. In His parable of the wheat and the tares (Mt. 13) It is the "best of times and the worst of times". God's good harvest will come at a time when evil is also at its ripest and fullest on the earth.

The end of the age will be characterized by the ripening of the devil's harvest of evil and darkness **and** the Lord's harvest of good and light. We tend to focus too often on the harvest of evil; how bad the world is becoming, how moral standards are declining etc. etc., We should certainly be concerned, but we should refuse to be despondent, for Jesus has said that *"When you see these things begin to happen look up and lift up your heads, because your redemption is drawing near."* (Luke 21:28)

God's Three Harvests

Harvest time is not a time for speculation. The observation of the signs of the time should spur us to action and focus God's harvest at the end of the age is in three areas.

These three harvests are

1) the harvest of the fullness of God's work *in* us

2) the harvest of His work among the nations (global evangelization)

3) His harvest in the political, historical order which is shown in the regathering of the Jews to their land and the aligning of the nations for His return. This turns our hearts and prayers towards Jerusalem and to the return of the Lord. (Psalm 122:6)

The evangelization of the nations, the building up of Israel and the rising of the glory of the Lord on His people (faithful Israel and the believers) in the eyes of the Lord are all one great movement from heaven. His great harvest.

The Harvest In Us

The purpose of the gospel is not simply to fill the earth with forgiven sinners, but to transform sons of Adam into sons of God. It is the power of God to cause us to be fully transformed into the image and likeness of a Jesus.

Jesus came to be the first of many brothers. His plan is to fill the earth with millions of men and women walking with God as He walked with God. He wants us to be filled with *"all the fullness of God"* (Ephesians 3:19)

He calls us to be in the world as Jesus (1 John 4.17), to love as He loved (John. 13.34), to walk as He walked (1 John. 2:6) and to do the

works that He did (John 14.12). All of this is possible through
- absolute surrender to the Lordship of Jesus, and
- to the will of the Father
- being totally emptied of self, pride and ego and
- utterly filled with the fullness of the Holy Spirit.

Now is the time for this harvest to be produced on the earth. The Word, the Spirit and the Cross are working together in the lives of believers to produce s harvest of the fullness of God's life in us. An incredible call goes out to the believers of this generation: to give ourselves to live as agents of God's love wisdom and compassion.

Paul's prayer for the Ephesians was that they would be *"filled with the fullness of God "* (Eph. 3.19) In the same letter he declares that the purpose of the ministry offices was to help to bring us to *"the measure of the stature of the fullness of Christ"* (Eph. 4.13). We can build on the great foundational doctrines of Grace, the Love of God and New Birth.... but not stop there. *"Therefore leaving (i.e. building on) the elementary doctrines let us go on to perfection".* (Hebrews 6:1) Now more than every we should also give ourselves to live and serve as Christ did in the world. *"Christ suffered for us leaving us an example that you should follow in His steps"* (1 Peter 2.21). The call go out to the end time generation to give ourselves to be like Jesus in the world as agents of love compassion and good ness. A tremendous harvest will be reaped *through* us when the Lord's harvest of compassion and goodness is ripened *in* us.

Daniel saw that, in the end of the age, there would be an explosion in information and travel and evil would increase: *"but the people that do know their God shall be strong, and do exploits."* (Daniel 11:32)

The Global Harvest

The second area of the harvest is the harvest of global evangelism. The end of the age is the time when the Lord will reap His harvest among the nations. When Jesus spoke of the harvest He spoke especially of the harvest of souls to be won from the nations. *"The harvest is great but the laborers are few pray therefore for the Lord of the harvest to send laborers into the harvest field."* (Luke 10:2)

The Lord of the harvest is summoning each of us to be in some way or another active in the harvest. To be a harvester, one does not necessarily have to go to far off lands. The harvest is at each one of our doorsteps. It is the neighbor next door, the co-worker in the hospital, the acquaintance in prison, etc. We can all be involved in the harvest with our prayer, our time our help and our focus.

When He sent His disciples into all the world He also gave them authority also. *"All authority has been given to me in heaven and on earth. Go therefore and make disciples of all the nations .. and lo I am with you always even to the end of the age."* (Mt 28:18-20) Even as He gave this great commission, Jesus' mind was on *this* season of harvest, the end of the age.

Authority And Harvest

Authority and harvest go together. Since we are now in the end of the age it is the time for us to recover the *authority* that is given to us as believers. This is what is happening all over the world. As the word of God is proclaimed in greater fullness believers are recovering and exercising their authority in prayer and in word and deed.

When Jesus sent out the disciples He gave them authority over *"all the works of the enemy."* (Luke 10) They returned from their mission amazed at the wonderful things that had happened at their hands. Jesus said: *"Do not rejoice that the demons are subject to you but rejoice because your names are written in heaven."* (Luke 10:20)

The Gospel Of The Kingdom

As the season of the harvest is upon us we proclaim not only the gospel of grace but also the gospel of the kingdom. We proclaim not only the gospel of the merciful forgiveness of God through Jesus and our reconciliation with God, but also proclaim the gospel of the Lordship of the Messiah and our submission to His Lordship. The task of worldwide evangelism is not only to proclaim to all men the forgiveness of sins through the Atoning sacrifice, but to bring men out from the oppressive dominion of the devil and in under the Lordship of Jesus and into the abundant life of God's Kingdom.

Jesus, the Great Harvester said "the thief comes to steal kill and destroy but I am come that they may have life and have it more abundantly." (Jn. 10:10) He did not upbraid the oppressed of this world, - He rescued them. Today's harvesters have a

Harvesters do not go into the world in a spirit of self-righteous correction. They go as the Father sent Jesus, with compassion.

motivation of compassion rather than of correction. Harvesters do not go into the world in a spirit of self-righteous correction. They go as the Father sent Jesus, with compassion, in the Spirit of Jesus.

Jesus is already Lord, of all the nations - the devil's authority is broken. It remains for us to simply recognize that it is broken, shake it off and walk away from it by placing ourselves under the Lordship of Jesus. In these harvest days all over the world, believers are proclaiming to the oppressed people of the earth that this authority is broken. Millions are being liberated through the Good News from the devil's illegal oppression, and coming to freedom and blessing in Christ.. *"The Spirit of the Lord GOD is upon me, because the LORD has anointed me to bring good tidings to the afflicted; He has sent me to bind up the brokenhearted, to proclaim liberty to the captives, and the opening of the prison to those who are bound."* (Isaiah 61:1)

Harvest Of History

God has a plan for the fullness of time to unite all things in Christ things and bring everything on earth under His dominion. (Ephesians 1:10) All earth will come under loving rule. *"Every knee shall bow and every tongue confess that Jesus Christ is Lord, to the glory of God the Father."* (Philippians 2:11)

"For when the Lord will build up Zion, He will appear in His glory." It is evident we are at the time when the Lord is building up Zion (Psalm 102:16). But the news is not all good, for Isaiah tells us that the time of the appearing of

the Lord's glory in Israel will be a time of deep darkness on the earth. *"Arise shine for your light is come and the glory of the Lord is risen upon you For behold the darkness shall cover the earth and deep darkness the people; but the Lord will arise over you and His glory will be seen upon you."* (Isaiah 60:1-4) This corresponds exactly to Jesus' parable of the harvest of the wheat and tares in Matthew 13. The drawing in of the Gentiles to the light of the gospel comes at the time of the rising of God's glory on Zion and the gathering of the people of Israel to the land. So, Israel is the trigger of the end time move of God's glory and the drawing in of Gentiles to the light.

Unfortunately, we have had some poor end-time teaching in the church. God's plan is not to "blow up" the world and send Jesus to take all the saints away to heaven. He has a plan to **redeem** the creation and to set up His throne on earth in Jerusalem. He has a plan to bring heaven to earth as He taught us to pray: *"Thy Kingdom come on earth as it is heaven."*

> God's plan is not to destroy the earth but to redeem it!

Though the end of the age will be a time of darkness as well as a time of light. It will be a time of shaking among the nations and wars and rumors of wars. Yet our message to the world is not one of doom and gloom. It is one of great hope - what Paul calls "The Blessed Hope."" For the grace of God has appeared for the salvation of all men, training us to renounce irreligion and worldly passions, and to live sober, upright, and godly lives in this world, *awaiting our **blessed hope**, the appearing of the glory of our great God and Savior Jesus Christ,* (Titus 2:13)

We have a message of extraordinary hope not only for ourselves but also for the whole creation. For Jesus is returning not only to complete our redemption but to inaugurate the golden age of peace upon the earth. *"They shall not hurt or destroy in all my holy mountain; for the earth shall be full of the knowledge of the LORD as the waters cover the sea."* (Habakkuk 2:13)

The church has focused on *individual* redemption while virtually ignoring God's plan for *world* redemption. This has caused some to be preoccupied with personal *survival* rather than on the bringing of God's kingdom to the earth. Yes the Lord is coming back and we will rise to meet Him , but not to *escape* this hopeless world. We will rise to meet Him and welcome Him back as the Redeemer, Healer of the planet and King of Jerusalem and of the world.

His return will fulfill His promise to Israel and to the Church and bring peace from Jerusalem to Israel and the world.

"Now it shall come to pass in the last days
that the mountain of the Lord's house
Shall be established on the top of the
mountains,
And shall be exalted above the hills
And all nations shall flow to it.
Many people shall come and say:
"Come and let us go up to the mountain of the
Lord
to the house of the God of Jacob; He will teach
of His ways,
And we shall walk in His paths."
For out of Zion shall go forth the law,
And the word of the Lord from Jerusalem.
He shall judge between the nations,
And rebuke many people;
They shall beat their swords into plowshares,
And their spears into pruning hooks;
Nation shall not lift up sword against nation,
Neither shall they learn war anymore." (Is: 2)

        The present flow of history will climax in the triumphant coming (return) of Jesus the Messiah to fulfill God's promises to Israel and the church. When He came the First time He inaugurated the New Covenant and atoned for the sins of the world. At that time Many of the Jewish people failed to recognize Him as the Messiah because He did not assert Himself as the triumphant heir to David's throne ruling from Jerusalem. This He will do at His Second

Coming. *"This same Jesus who was taken up from you into heaven, will so come in like manner as you saw Him go into heaven."* (Acts 1:10) He will return again to occupy the throne of David and to rule the earth from Jerusalem - the Lion of the Tribe of Judah.

God has a plan for the *fullness of times* to replace the kingdoms of this world with the kingdoms of the Messiah. *"Then the seventh angel blew his trumpet, and there were loud voices in heaven, saying, "The kingdoms of this world has become the kingdoms of our Lord and of His Christ, and He shall reign for ever and ever."* (Rev. 11:15).

God' s plan for the ***fullness of times*** plan is not to destroy the earth but to replace the kingdoms of this world with the kingdoms of the Messiah and to turn this earth into a paradise again. (Rev. 11:15). The efforts of the nations to bring peace and justice to the earth have failed, but the Lord will replace the present world order with the rule of Jesus and His bride

A tremendous golden age is ahead for this planet. It will manifest soon when the failed human systems of the earth will be replaced by glorious, loving, benign and powerful rule of Jesus the Messiah of Israel and the world.

"There shall come forth a shoot from the stump of Jesse, and a branch shall grow out of his roots.

And the Spirit of the LORD shall rest upon Him , the spirit of wisdom and understanding, the spirit of counsel and might, the spirit of knowledge and the fear of the LORD.

And His delight shall be in the fear of the LORD.

He shall not judge by what His eyes see, or decide by what His ears hear;

but with righteousness he shall judge the poor, and decide with equity for the meek of the earth;

and he shall smite the earth with the rod of His mouth,

and with the breath of His lips he shall slay the wicked.

Righteousness shall be the girdle of His waist, and faithfulness the girdle of His loins.

The wolf shall dwell with the lamb, and the leopard shall lie down with the kid, and the calf and the lion and the fatling together, and a little child shall lead them.

The cow and the bear shall feed; their young shall lie down together; and the lion shall eat straw like the ox.

The sucking child shall play over the hole of the asp, and the weaned child shall put His hand on the adder's den.

They shall not hurt or destroy in all my holy mountain; for the earth shall be full of the knowledge of the LORD as the waters cover the sea. (Isa 11:1-9)

At this time, our responsibility is to be

awake, to know "the signs of the times" and not be asleep. We lay hold of our calling to be like Jesus, take our part in the harvest and joyfully anticipate the glorious time that is coming to us and to the world when Jesus returns to bring in the millennial age of global peace harmony and fruitfulness.

Are you ready!

AFTERWORD

G od's love is not a religion. The demands of love cannot be contained in any religious formula. Real Christianity is not a religion but a life of loving God, being loved by Him and loving others. The expression that love will take is different for all of us, but the principle is the same.

Many accept the love of God but do not want the inconvenience of loving others. Loving others in the context of our homes, our work and our church can be at times extremely inconvenient but the rewards are great. The "death to self involved in being willing to love and serve when inconvenient is true Christianity. A generation of followers of Jesus is rising on the earth today who refuse to be bound by selfishness, unforgiveness and partisan tradition. They are determined, not merely to serve religion but to see and know the living God.

Once we are reconciled with God, as we have seen, God implants His own nature in us by the Holy Spirit. Our only responsibility now is to remain in union with this new nature so that

God's love can continue to be expressed through us.

God is not looking for religious people, but ordinary people who will receive His forgiveness, His nature and in turn forgive and bless others. The message demands a response. Will yours be "Yes Lord!"?

PRAYER FOR A NEW BEGINNING
(NEW LIFE)

Dear Heavenly Father,

I come to You today just as I am. I acknowledge that I am a sinner in need of Your salvation. I believe that on the Cross, Your Son, Jesus, died and took on Himself my guilt, shame and blame, and atoned for all my sins. I believe that He rose from the dead for my justification and opened up for me right standing with You. I put my faith in this fact and I accept Your forgiveness and reconciliation. I also in return forgive all who have injured and hurt me.

I lay down the sinful, selfish side of my nature and I ask You, Jesus to live in my heart by Your Spirit as my new "engine for living". Live in my heart, love through my heart, see through my eyes, speak through my lips, touch through my hands, and walk this earth in my body.

I formally acknowledge You as my Lord and Savior and ask you to be the Managing Director of the rest of my life. I trust You to empower me by Your Spirit to live by Your way.

By this I seal my covenant with You and confess that I am born-again and reconciled to God through Jesus' Blood.

Thank you God, My Heavenly Father, for accepting me as Your child and adopting me into Your family.

To order more copies of
Christianity Without Religion
write to Reconciliation Outreach
P.O. Box 2778, Stuart, FL 34995, USA
Or e-mail: paulandnuala@bellsouth.net
Or go to www.reconciliationoutreach.net

You can help us with our ministry of good news by making sure that your local Christian bookstore and library carries this book and other books by Paul & Nuala O'Higgins

More Books by Paul & Nuala O'Higgins
- The Supernatural Habits Of The Spirit Empowered Believer
- Good News In Israel's Feasts
- New Testament Believer's & The Law
- The Four Great Covenants
- In Israel Today With Yeshua
- Have You Received The Holy Spirit?
- Life Changing World Changing Prayer

ABOUT THE AUTHORS

Paul and Nuala O'Higgins are natives of Ireland who reside in Stuart Florida. They are the directors of Reconciliation Outreach – a ministry of teaching and interdenominational evangelism.

In full-time ministry together since 1977 they have ministered in over thirty nations. Nuala's degree is in education and Paul's degrees are in Philosophy and Theology. He holds a doctorate in Biblical Theology.

They are heralds of the love of God made available by the Cross. Their call is to make known the treasures of God's kingdom and equip believers to be more effective followers of Jesus.